SURVIVOR

The fortunate story of a Radio Officer from Hull in the Merchant Navy during WW2

by

Melvin Stringer

Grosvenor House
Publishing Limited

This book is published by
Grosvenor House Publishing Ltd
Link House
140 The Broadway, Tolworth, Surrey, KT6 7HT.
www.grosvenorhousepublishing.co.uk

A CIP record for this book
is available from the British Library

Hardback ISBN 978-1-83615-409-9

For my children

Joanna

Lynsey

Alex

and for all who served in the Merchant Navy in WW2

Contents

Acknowledgements

I would like to express my thanks and appreciation to my wife Sue for the time and effort she has spent assisting me with proofreading and editing this book. She has always supported and encouraged me with my research and fact-finding for this project, to help me to bring this book to completion.

I am grateful to Grant Kemp from Restoring Your Past, for his work in colourising many photos, bringing them to life and ensuring they meet the requirements for printing quality.

For digitising my 16mm film of the Arandora Star from 1939, to enable me to capture still photos from it to use in this book, I would like to thank George Smith of G.H.S. Media.

Thanks go to Jerry Mason U.S.N. (ret) for translating the logs of U-123 on U-Boat.net and to Cristiano D'Adamo from regiamarina.net. I also appreciate the advice and information I have gained from many contributors on several Merchant Navy websites over the last 20 years.

Finally, it was a delight to come across Stuart Clayton, whose father Arthur Clayton served alongside my father Jack on the Holmbury. Stuart provided me with additional details, that only he and his brother knew about, from their father's time on the Holmbury.

Any inconsistencies, inaccuracies or errors are my own.

INTRODUCTION

In the summer of 1975, I was on holiday with my parents in Yorkshire, visiting my father's family who came from Hull. One afternoon, we had an outing to the picturesque fishing village of Robin Hood's Bay, 60 miles north of Hull. My father Jack decided he would like to try to find one of the captains he had sailed with during the war, as he had got on particularly well with him, and he remembered that the captain had lived in Robin Hood's Bay. His name was John Lawson, and he had been the captain of the cargo ship SS Holmbury when it was torpedoed in May 1943, off the West African coast. Captain Lawson was taken prisoner in the U-Boat that had destroyed his ship, and Jack had last seen him briefly in London, fifteen years earlier. Although Jack recalled that John Lawson had lived in this village, he could not remember the address. So, we went to one of the old red telephone boxes and flicked through the local directories that were always in there. Spotting the name Lawson, Jack dialled the number, and a woman answered, confirming she was the wife of John. Unfortunately, he had passed away a few years earlier, but she insisted we should come and see her as we were so close by.

Ten minutes later we were inside Mrs. Lawson's house, where Jack had a long chat with her, catching up with each other's lives, whilst I was volunteered to remove an old large bush from the back garden. An hour or so later, following tea, we were about to leave when Mrs. Lawson said she had something to give Jack. She produced the unique set of photographs which had been taken from the U-Boat, showing the sinking of the Holmbury and her husband John being taken on board the submarine as a prisoner. Mrs Lawson explained that the captain of the U-Boat had sent these photos to her husband John after the war. Immediately, I could see my father being transported back in time over 30 years, and from that moment a glimpse of what he had faced during the war became apparent to me. I would spend the rest of his life trying to glean as much information as I could about his experiences, although it was mostly towards the end of his life that he offered greater details.

Discovering more of his artefacts after his death spurred me on to create a more thorough story of his time in the Merchant Navy. This led me to many years of research, both online and through visiting places he had been to around the country, including Methil Docks which is just 20 miles from where I now live in Fife. This book is my attempt to show the unrelenting dangers and pressures that the Merchant Navy faced during nearly six years of conflict, through the experiences of one young man.

- **CUSTODY**

  When the ship is at sea, this book is to be kept in the Radio Office. In a harbour, the Master is personally responsible for its custody.

- **DESTRUCTION**

  If the ship is in danger of sinking or capture or if it becomes necessary to scuttle the ship, this book is to be thrown overboard in the metal box provided in the Radio Office. Where this equipment is not carried, the book is to be destroyed by burning if possible; otherwise it should be put in a weighted bag equipped with grommets to admit water readily and thrown overboard in deep water.

From WIMS Radio Manual (Wartime Instructions for Merchant Ships)
Admiralty London

Chapter 1
SS Arandora Star

Jack Stringer wandered across the wide deserted observation deck at the top of the luxury cruise liner, the SS Arandora Star, and looked down from the railings, forty feet above the quayside. In contrast to the usual loading regime of porters carrying suitcases and trunks, he noticed with surprise that soldiers were sliding wooden boxes off an adjacent railway truck. With military precision, they proceeded to carry them on board, via the wooden gangway. Taking out a packet of Players cigarettes he pulled one out, struck a match and lit it, then tried to make sense of the picture evolving below him, and the events of the last few weeks. As the sun began to climb to start another late summer's day in Southampton Docks, it was 6.45 on Friday morning the 1st of September 1939.

The Arandora Star had steamed back into her home port of Southampton the previous Saturday evening, the 26th of August, having been suddenly ordered to cut short her three-week cruise around Iceland and Scandinavia by one week, due to the worsening crisis with Germany. The following day, the Admiralty ordered the Mediterranean Sea temporarily closed to British Merchant shipping and redirected all other shipping, including the fishing fleet.

Preparations for war had been gaining ground rapidly over the previous weeks, from the call-up of reservists to testing of blackout procedures, from restricting food shopping to the start of the evacuation of children from cities - which was commencing this very morning. Radio and newspaper reports were increasingly recounting stories from across Europe, of Germans and other nationalities heeding the call to return home, but cancellations and re-routing of passenger ships were adding to the chaos. Cross-channel ferries and planes were packed, and most non-Europeans were desperately trying to acquire accommodation on trans-Atlantic routes, to return to their own countries.

To add to the growing tension in England, the IRA (Irish Republican Army) had recently increased its bombing campaign during the year, with a series of bombings utilising tradesmen's bicycles which they left outside public buildings. The IRA caused explosions in Coventry, Liverpool and Blackpool, hoping to take advantage of the growing international crisis and demands on the authorities.

As Jack watched the Military Police counting the boxes onto his ship, he wondered if he might be completing his last cruise as an assistant purser. Having just celebrated his nineteenth birthday a few days before, his life was about to change forever.

It had been an eventful start to his adult life, having left Malet Lambert School in Hull fewer than eighteen months ago. Hull was a city with a population of 320,000 and was still trying to recover from the depression, with limited opportunities available. The dockyard area was still the heart of the city. The Ellerman's Wilson Line had one of the biggest fleets in the world with

105 ships, and Hull was one of their most significant ports. The influence of the sea on the city of Hull had led the 17-year-old Jack, in April 1938, to apply (and be accepted) for the job as a Junior Assistant Purser with the Canadian Pacific Steamship Company. Following several trips to Montreal in Canada serving on board the liners SS Duchess of Richmond and SS Montrose during his first year in work, he successfully applied to the Blue Star Line in March 1939, to work on the Arandora Star. With a promotion to Assistant Purser, he was proud to have become the youngest purser ever with the Blue Star Line and was looking confidently to the future.

The Arandora Star was a highly respected luxury cruise ship, built in 1927, accommodating just 354 passengers, all travelling first class. She was widely known as the "Wedding Cake" or the "Chocolate Box" due to her white hull with its scarlet ribbon, and she became a favourite with the rich and famous. As Jack looked down below, over the games deck, he remembered the various activities that had taken place there: the tennis matches and treasure hunts, the children's egg and spoon races, the sack races, the gentlemen's balloon races – which led to great hilarity. He remembered how impressed he had been when he first stepped aboard the ship six months ago. There was the sumptuous Louis XIV style dining room and the elegant ballroom (which held the fancy-dress dinners and dances), the smoking room, cinema and swimming pool, and there was such a high standard of accommodation and cuisine. An additional bonus was the photographic darkroom to enable a quick processing of photographs, which Jack took advantage of.

His memory flashed through all the new ports and cities he had visited on the cruises earlier that year around the Mediterranean and Scandinavia. He had a special recollection of witnessing the land of the midnight sun, with 24 hours of daylight in the Arctic Circle. He was grateful for all he had experienced, the variety of people he had met during this period, and how his life had already changed.

As he finished his cigarette, the sound of shunting from the railway waggons below told Jack the mysterious cargo had now been stored safely. He crossed the deck, walking past the gymnasium, glancing at the rows of other ships in the packed docks, noticing yet another liner being guided into a nearby berth by two tugs. Jack knew this was going to be a hectic day, as the ship had become fully booked immediately after the announcement had been made a few days ago, of their changed plans to now depart for New York. This was going to be a new destination, not only for Jack but also for the ship and many of the crew who had never been there before.

Just before 7am, he headed down the wide central staircase, proceeding into the heart of the ship, three decks below. He passed the ship's shop on his way to the Pursers' Office with its large, curved mahogany counter, for the start of his duties. The ship was alive with cleaners and stewards passing by, trying to re-stock and put the finishing touches to over two hundred cabins, plus numerous function rooms. The high level of service on board was carried out by one hundred and sixty stewards, eighteen cooks, six bakers, three butchers, a five-piece band, a surgeon and a hairdresser plus two shop attendants, making up the total crew number to around two hundred and fifty.

Under the very experienced senior purser, Hugh Pease, who had been with the ship throughout its time at sea, Jack and his three other colleagues would spend the next few hours finalising the full list of passengers, which was constantly changing. That morning the papers were already reporting that several hundred Americans were stuck in Glasgow desperately trying to get passage back home, just one of many instances of what was happening in the major ports of Britain.

Messages of requests and cancellations were relentlessly coming into the office, as passengers had difficulties travelling to Southampton. Trains were delayed due to the start of the mass evacuation of children from London, known as Operation Pied Piper, the four-day movement of children away from the capital and other major cities. Many passengers had therefore opted to travel by road, and several of the main roads were being turned into one-way routes out of the capital to speed up the evacuation process. Little did anyone know yet, but the German invasion of Poland had already started at 4.45 that morning, heralding the beginning of another world war.

Under the supervision of the head steward, additional beds were also being provided, as after the Arandora Star docked later that day at Cherbourg in Northern France for additional passengers, the revised total number of 441 passengers would become a record. Following breakfast at 8am the whole ship's company mustered, wearing their lifebelts to be checked at their designated stations, before they practised lifeboat drill for a possible evacuation. Back in the office to check their stock of American and European currencies for exchange, the pursers, along with the rest of the crew, were ready to begin the embarkation of passengers from 10.30am.

Once through border checks the steady stream of 284 passengers commenced boarding. As expected, most of them were American, ranging from merchants, bankers, businessmen, engineers, lawyers, professors and students, to artists, secretaries, housewives and children. Britons, Canadians, Australians and a smattering of other nationals from China, Japan, India and South America completed the mix. As many had stayed the night in some of the most central London hotels such as the Regents Palace and Strand Palace, or the most exclusive including the Waldorf, Savoy and Claridge's, it was clear the wealthy had an advantage gaining passage home.

Included amongst the passengers boarding was Mr George Richter, 64, with his wife and daughter. He was a well-known American art historian, specialising in European art, who was taking a keen interest in the safety of his library of 60,000 photographs of art and architecture accompanying him. It is worth noting that in 1943, following his death the previous year, the George M. Richter Archive of Illustrations on Art became the founding set of photographs in the image collection at the Washington National Gallery of Art.

Another passenger was Dennis Puleston, 34, who although born in England was setting off for a new life in America with his wife. He was a man of many talents being a wildlife artist, an adventurer and a naval architect, who had already spent six years sailing around the world. Three years later, in 1942, he helped develop and then train personnel using the DUKW, the army's amphibious landing craft used in the Normandy landings, the Mediterranean and Pacific, being injured in the Far East doing so. After the war he was the prime activist in proving that the use of the chemical DDT (dichloro-diphenyl-trichloroethane) to eradicate mosquitoes was causing huge losses to birds and wildlife, and his actions successfully got it banned in America in 1972.

Amongst the nineteen young children on board were Elizabeth and Robert Montgomery, aged six and three respectively, accompanied by their nanny. Their father, Robert Montgomery was a well-known American actor who was in England at the time, making a film. He was now planning to join the American Field Service attached to the French Army, as an ambulance driver, and his wife was going to join the Red Cross. The children were due to board another ship, the SS Athenia, which was leaving from Glasgow that day via Liverpool to Canada. However, a mix up with the booking probably saved the lives of the children due to events two days later. The young Elizabeth Montgomery would go on to lead a very successful film and television career, especially during the 1960s and 1970s when she starred as the loveable witch Samantha, in the comedy series Bewitched.

These would have just appeared as normal passengers for Jack, knowing nothing about their backgrounds, however he couldn't fail to notice one of the last groups to arrive on board. Sweeping through the corridors, the 31-year-old Maharaja (King), Bir Bikram Manikya of Tripura (a princely state in North-East India), dressed impeccably in a pin-striped suit, trilby hat and silver handled walking cane, smiled broadly at his fellow passengers. His entourage of eight attendants, his secretary and staff officer, followed by several porters, was greeted by 53-year-old Captain Moulton, who had commanded the ship for the past 10 years. As the group stopped by the Pursers' office, the Captain introduced Mr. Pease who held one of the keys for the ship's safe where their valuables could be left for safekeeping. Then they were directed to the deck below where they had been allocated several adjoining suites.

At 12.45pm, with the sun shining brightly, the Arandora Star slipped its last mooring rope, and two tugs assisted the ship away from the quayside, as a long blast of the ship's whistle sounded its departure. Whilst the sound and vibration of the engines increased, along with the smoke from the twin funnels, several excited passengers waved at the dock workers, instead of members of the public who would have usually seen off the ship. Gradually increasing speed, the Arandora Star made her way down Southampton Water and the deep channel, to sail east around the Isle of Wright towards France. During the crossing, the first pieces of information regarding Germany's invasion of Poland started to become public knowledge on the ship, following Hitler's speech broadcast at around 11am, as this information was relayed by the shipping company in London. As a result, the passengers paid more attention than usual to the mustering in the public rooms at 6pm with their lifebelts and instructions about evacuation procedures, before they headed off to their substantial evening meal.

As the sun started to set, the Arandora Star passed through the outer breakwaters of Cherbourg Harbour in Normandy, then the inner walls, to berth at the quayside at 7.40pm. Most of the additional passengers now boarding were, again, from North America, many having cut short their holidays in Europe on advice from their embassy. Also noticeable to Jack, the passenger list showed several passengers from Austria and Germany who were registered as stateless, but hoping for a new life in the U.S.A.

Two and a half hours later, in darkness, the Arandora Star was guided back into the English Channel, before heading west towards the Atlantic Ocean. The talk on board was now all about the invasion of Poland, and how the governments in Britain and France would respond, bearing in mind their joint agreement to come to Poland's aid if the country was attacked. During this time of fast changing events, just three days after the Arandora Star departed, the advance party of the British Expeditionary Force landed here at Cherbourg. As the outline of the French coastline disappeared from view, the passengers gradually drifted off to bed. Having familiarised themselves with the ship or taken a last drink or a stroll along the deck promenade, an over-riding feeling of relief prevailed, that they were leaving Europe behind. For Jack, he was glad to finally get to bed around midnight, but he had come to the conclusion that the next planned cruise around the Mediterranean, due in just over three weeks' time, would now never happen.

During the following day, the Arandora Star began to, at least outwardly, resume the usual appearance and feel of a normal cruise, as the late summer warm weather continued. The swimming pool proved popular, especially with the children, the deck games commenced, and as the passengers enjoyed the first-class facilities on board, they started to get to know each other and swap stories.

However, news reports were picked up and passed on to their fellow travellers, by those passengers who had brought expensive portable radios on board with them. Both the British and French Governments had now informed the German authorities that the German forces must immediately withdraw from Poland, or they would honour their agreement to come to Poland's aid, but no reply had been forthcoming. On the contrary, reports stated that German forces were bombing more cities and penetrating further into Poland, and the news continued to report of the increased readiness for war in Europe.

In the early evening, sitting in the Pursers' office, Jack and his colleagues were discussing some of the more unusual news items from the conversations they had had earlier with the passengers. Apparently, London Zoo would be destroying their venomous animals for safety reasons, in case the buildings got bombed and they escaped, while some of the larger animals were being relocated to Whipsnade Park. One elderly passenger with connections to London Zoo had a list of zoo animals that could be sponsored and planned to contribute to the upkeep of two sea lions at £12 per month. As this was a month's pay for Jack and his colleagues, they checked her list and responded that they would consider taking on a dormouse at four shillings a month between them.

Following another evacuation drill with all the passengers, the evening progressed in much the same way as during Jack's previous cruises, with the Captain and some of the senior officers in their crisp white uniforms attending the five-course evening meal with the passengers. Afterwards, the sounds of the five-piece band playing a repertoire of waltzes, foxtrots and quicksteps, drifted down to the pursers' office from the ballroom on the deck above. As Jack looked forward to the end of his shift, passengers relaxed in one of the lounges, played cards, watched a film at the cinema, or gazed at the churning wake from the sheltered aft deck. As the brightly lit ship made steady progress through the Atlantic darkness, no one on board could have imagined this scene would not be repeated for several years.

The following morning, Sunday the 3rd of September, commenced with the usual substantial breakfast served in the dining room. A religious service from a travelling American minister was available for those who wished to attend, and the passengers relaxed in the sunshine, looking forward to lunch. Suddenly, the Tannoy system broadcast that there was to be a special announcement from the Captain in five minutes, at midday. As the passengers gathered in small groups it seemed the whole ship came to a standstill in anticipation of this moment.

"Ladies and gentlemen, this is Captain Moulton speaking. At 11.15am today the British Prime minister, Neville Chamberlain, made the following announcement on the BBC Radio, which I will now read.

'This morning the British Ambassador in Berlin handed the German Government a final note stating that, unless we heard from them by 11 o'clock that they were prepared at once to withdraw their troops from Poland, a state of war would exist between us. I have to tell you now that no such undertaking has been received, and that consequently this country is at war with Germany......'

As a result of this news, and following instructions from the Admiralty, we will therefore be carrying out certain precautions, which may include altering our course. This could result in a slight delay to our arrival in New York, but you will be kept fully informed of this and the other measures we will be taking, after lunch. In the meantime, please be assured that you are quite safe, and we will endeavour to make the remainder of your voyage as pleasant as possible. Thank you for your time, and I will speak to you again shortly."

On board the ship, these instructions were introduced over the course of the day which brought home the reality of the declaration of war. Blackout notices were put up throughout the ship warning passengers not to smoke after dusk whilst on deck. To prevent light escaping at night, sheets of canvas were cut and fitted around all deck doors, and all portholes, windows and deck glass were painted with dark blue paint. All lifeboat stores were double checked, and following messages from the Admiralty the ship began a more southerly course, considered to be safer from a possible U-Boat attack. Finally, the difficult task of painting the ship's superstructure from white to dark grey was started over the next couple of days, to conform to wartime regulations.

Despite the disruption on board, the passengers were generally understanding, although the main concern expressed to Jack and his colleagues was asking how much longer the journey was going to take now. Several requests were made to the pursers' office to send radio telegrams to inform relatives and interested parties, but these were forbidden under the new regulations. The pursers tried to reassure the more nervous passengers throughout the day that these were mere precautions, as news came through that France, India, Australia and New Zealand had joined Great Britain, in declaring war on Germany.

However, the general anxiety on board increased greatly, when the upsetting news filtered through late that evening and the following day that the first British ship had been torpedoed, on a parallel course heading for Canada. This was the passenger liner SS Athenia, which had left Liverpool the day before, the 2nd of September, for Montreal. On board were 1,103 passengers, three-quarters of whom were women and children, including 500 Jewish refugees. At 17.40 hours on Sunday the 3rd of September, she was hit by a torpedo from the German submarine U30, about 200 miles northwest of Northern Ireland.

Although rescue vessels were relatively quickly on hand, 93 passengers and 19 crew died, and among the dead were 28 US citizens. Due to fears that this might bring America into the war, Germany denied involvement, altered their submarine's logbook, and promptly blamed the British for the sinking, trying to turn neutral countries against them. It was not until after the end of the war, at the Nuremburg Trials, that the truth was revealed by the German Navy. At the time, the Arandora Star was around 600 miles south of the stricken vessel and began to zigzag her way across the Atlantic to avoid a similar fate.

Two further lifeboat drills were held for passengers over the next two days highlighting the concerns of those on board, following reports of several other merchant ships being sunk in the Atlantic. It was also noticeable that several of the crew members were positioned around the upper decks, taking shifts of scanning the sea with binoculars. The passengers' portable radios were not confiscated, which surprised Jack, because he was aware that the radios' signals could possibly lead to the ship's location being detected by the enemy. Some of the woman on board even began to stay up all night with their jewellery and other valuables close by, ready to abandon ship if necessary.

To try to lighten the mood, the crew and some of the passengers carried out practical jokes on the more gullible. One evening, a young teenage American student, Virginia Lovel, appeared at the pursers' counter.

"I've just been speaking to some passengers during dinner, and they said I should put my name down for a lifeboat reservation as soon as possible."

Quick as a flash one of Jack's colleagues replied, whilst checking some papers he held.

"Oh dear, we're very sorry Miss Lovell, all the lifeboat reservations have been taken. However, we do still have a couple of prime spots left on the rafts, if you would like one."

"Oh, yes please, that would be great, I'll let my friends know too," she responded, as she rushed back up the corridor to finish her meal.

On the 6th of September, Captain Moulton made another announcement stating that the hot water would be turned off for the time being, and the crew would be loosening the lifeboats on the top deck, for safety reasons. He also announced that their expected arrival in New York would be Monday evening on the 11th of September, rather than the previous morning.

Despite this disappointing news, the passengers and crew tried to continue enjoying themselves. The gala nights, dancing and deck games went ahead as planned, although the rooms became rather stuffy due to the restricted ventilation. However, down in the engine rooms the fifteen firemen, working in shifts, sweated continuously in the stifling temperatures, as they ensured the boilers maintained the ship's maximum speed of 16 knots. They were more aware than most that if the ship was hit by a torpedo, they would have little chance of survival. The main preoccupation on board was now watching the sea for signs of the enemy, and there were several false alarms made by some of the more nervous passengers.

Finally, on Monday the 11th of September, the Captain announced that they had reached American waters, and the relief was immense. A flurry of requests was made at the pursers' office for messages to be sent by the ship's radio operators to inform the passengers' relatives of their safe arrival, none being more relieved than the Montgomery children's parents, back in England. A celebration dinner was organised for that evening, and the drinks flowed as the Canadian passengers on board generously joined together and paid for a round of drinks for everyone, as they learnt that their country had also entered the war on the Allied side.

As the liner crept slowly into New York harbour on a warm evening, dropping anchor just after midnight, the dancing and drinking was still in full swing. The passengers and crew were finally allowed on deck to continue the party, and the deck lights were switched on. Several people had tears in their eyes, as they gazed at the brightly lit silhouette of the city ahead of them and toasted their safe arrival. For a few minutes, Jack went outside with his colleagues to take in the panorama of the largest city in the world, as he looked forward to exploring its vibrant life.

In bright sunshine the following morning, the Arandora Star gently edged up the bay. At 9.30am the ship finally moored at Cunard's West Fourteenth Street Pier, in the heart of Manhattan, 45 hours after her expected arrival. Despite a few hangovers from the previous night's celebrations, final bills for passengers were dealt with in the busy pursers' office, then shortly afterwards the passengers streamed down the gangway onto the quay and into the huge adjacent immigration hall. They were closely followed by lines of stewards and porters, who were delighted to receive some very large tips for transporting piles of luggage. Two armoured lorries, with several police motorbike escorts, then pulled in next to the ship and boxes were manhandled into them, under the gaze of about ten guards with machine guns. In less than an hour the vehicles had disappeared from the quayside with sirens blazing, into the heart of the city.

A few newspaper reporters started interviewing some of the passengers, after they had passed through customs and immigration control. Amongst them was the Maharaja of Tripura who forecast the war would be a long one. He pledged his support to the Empire in the war and said that other princes would stand behind Britain. Asked about his plans for getting home, the Maharaja confirmed that he and his contingent would be travelling across the United States to San Francisco, on route to India, as it had been impossible to get steamship accommodation through the shorter route via the Mediterranean. With that he wished everyone well, and his party climbed aboard the waiting taxis to continue their elongated journey.

The reporters were then allowed to board the ship to speak to some of the officers. Captain Moulton informed them that he was under Admiralty orders and could not discuss the voyage, so he left to go on shore to talk to the agent of the ship's company. However, Jack was with Hugh, the Chief Purser, when the reporters approached, and Hugh described the trip to them. To Jack's surprise, Hugh confirmed that they had also been carrying over $3,500,000 in gold bars from the Bank of England to the Federal Reserve in New York, (approximately £72,000,000 in value in 2024). This consignment of around 65 boxes, each containing four gold bars, was one of the first shipments of gold to go to the USA to pay for armaments for the war.

Hugh then mentioned that although the passengers were aware of a few other ships being attacked in the North Atlantic, in truth a total of fifteen British merchant vessels had already been sunk during their voyage. As Hugh took them all to the Captain's cabin to see the chart which indicated their route, and the reported submarine positions, Jack realised for the first time just how lucky they had been, to depart when they did.

Most of the crew drew some of their wages at the office and gratefully took some shore leave. Jack enjoyed some time later that afternoon with his colleagues, visiting the attractions among the towering skyscrapers in Manhattan, on an open top bus. A visit to the Rockefeller building for the city-wide views, drinks in a couple of bars and his first taste of hotdogs, was followed by an evening visit to the cavernous Roxy Theatre, with almost six thousand seats, to see the newly released film, The Adventures of Sherlock Holmes.

The following day, and with some disappointment as there was neither cargo nor passengers to take on board, preparations to depart commenced. Basic supplies were replenished, ballast tanks were opened, and the ship trimmed. Just over 30 hours after docking at New York, the Arandora Star slipped quietly away from its moorings at 5pm on Wednesday the 13th of September, minus one of the firemen who went AWOL (absent without official leave), deciding he was better off staying in the USA. Once out of American waters the Captain announced they were heading north under Admiralty orders to Halifax, Nova Scotia, in Canada, before returning to the UK. Blackout procedures were again enforced, and additional lookouts were posted as they headed north on a zigzag course, safely reaching their destination two days later in darkness at 22.40pm.

Halifax was established by the British in the mid-18th century, next to one of the world's deepest and widest natural ports. Being ice-free, with minimal tides, and strategically located closer to Europe than any other North American East Coast port, it also had the added advantage of the Bedford Basin. This is a large, enclosed bay, about three miles long and just under one mile wide, forming the northwestern end of Halifax Harbour. It provided an ideal protected anchorage, with good holding ground (mud) on the basin floor for around 150 ocean-going vessels. Following on from its use as a convoy assembly area in WW1, the harbour area was just starting to be prepared again for the same purpose, when the Arandora Star entered and dropped anchor in the Bedford Basin. At this point at the start of the war, the whole of the harbour was totally unprotected with no defensive armaments or anti-submarine netting, which would not be in place for another two months.

However, blissfully ignorant of this fact, as the crew surveyed their new surroundings in the morning light the following day, it was clear that several ships were gathering to form a convoy. Amongst them, Jack was delighted to notice the passenger liner the Duchess of Richmond, on which he had started his apprenticeship with cruises to Canada almost eighteen months previously. Jack and the crew then learned that just two days before their arrival at Halifax, and amid great concern and interest, a large crowd had gathered at the quayside. Together with over forty reporters, and many officials and dignitaries, the steamship City of Flint had docked with 223 survivors from the torpedoed SS Athenia. This was another reminder of the lucky voyage they had recently made.

Shore leave was granted for Saturday. Taking one of the ship's motor launches, Jack went to explore the town, but like most of his colleagues, he was disappointed, especially after the excitement of New York. Halifax had a population of around 67,000 at the time, and although this would almost double during the course of the war, it was a rather tired and faded seaport town, which had not recovered from the depression years. Therefore, it had little to offer sailors at that time, especially as there were no public drinking establishments. The recently enforced nighttime blackout regulations in town did little to lighten the mood.

Jack and his colleagues were able to watch from the quayside as a small piece of history unfolded in front of them. Fifteen British merchant vessels and three French vessels weighed anchor and slowly steamed out from the sheltered Bedford Basin. On board this first ever east bound convoy (HX.1) to the UK from North America, were a few of the varied range of cargoes that were necessary to keep Britain supplied, including diesel and crude oil, flour, wheat, tobacco, cotton, clay, lumber, pitch, coke, apples, ammunition and explosives. This hastily arranged convoy was escorted by the Canadian destroyers St. Laurent and Saguenay for just the first 350 miles. At that time, the Canadian Navy only possessed a total of six destroyers (four of which were in Halifax) plus a few minesweepers, so were unable to provide any greater protection. Offshore in the open seas of the North Atlantic, the British cruisers Berwick and York were awaiting convoy HX.1, but they could only stay with the convoy for one further day, due to other commitments. After this, the convoy was left on its own, averaging a slow and vulnerable 8 knots until it neared British waters.

Over the three full days the Arandora Star remained in Halifax, most of the remainder of the ship which had not yet been camouflaged was now also hurriedly painted in wartime regulation grey paint. This was hindered by a heavy downpour of rain all day on Sunday, and this situation was being repeated with several other passenger liners close by. Instructions were received for the Captain to attend a convoy conference on shore. Alongside one of the piers on Tuesday the 19th of September, 72 British passengers boarded for the return voyage back to the Arandora Star's home port of Southampton.

As they left the sheltered four-mile Halifax inlet that afternoon, the weather was warm and dry, and they were joined by the seven other passenger liners that had gathered recently in the Bedford Basin. These ships formed into two lines of four abreast as they encountered the swell from the Atlantic. Captain Moulton informed the crew that they were now part of HXF.1, the first fast convoy from Halifax heading to the UK. This included three modern French liners, the Champlain, Colombie and De Grasse, plus Jack's first liner the Duchess of Richmond, the Orbita and the Antonia. On either side of the convoy were the Canadian destroyers Fraser and Saguenay, the latter having just returned from escorting the first slow convoy (HX.1). Shortly afterwards, the returning British cruisers, Berwick and York, took up their stations at the front and rear, to proceed into the wide expanse of the ocean.

As the convoy ploughed through the seas at 15 knots, the crew felt a sense of comfort and pride as they watched this unique event unfold around them. Even when the escorts flashed their good luck messages on leaving the convoy after 24 hours, to return to Halifax for the next convoy forming, Jack felt secure within this group of fast, well-known trans-Atlantic liners. Now, with just a small number of passengers on board every effort was made to continue the high quality of food, service and leisure activities, albeit on a much quieter level. Additional lifeboat drills were carried out as before, together with the implementation of blackout regulations and restrictions during the night. These were necessary because the silhouettes and wakes of the speeding liners could be observed on the mainly clear evenings.

As each day passed, and they got closer to home without incident, the Arandora Star was slowly stripped of some of the fittings, paintings and ornaments in the 150 empty cabins. Jack and his colleagues created records of these items as they were stored away, leaving just essential furniture in place. The ship was rapidly losing its identity as a cruise liner and felt strangely empty without the usual volume of noise and requests from its wealthy passengers. The main rumour amongst the crew now, was that the ship was going to be used for troop transport, so talk of finding new employment, or getting called up for National Service, was constant. Of more immediate concern were the continuing attacks by U-Boats, particularly on the western approaches to Britain, where the convoy was heading. On the 17th of September they had heard the disturbing news that the aircraft carrier H.M.S. Courageous had been torpedoed, with the loss of over 500 of her crew. This was the first British warship to be sunk by German forces, occurring 150 miles southwest of the Irish coast.

In the ship's cinema, Jack did manage to watch some of the many excellent films released that year including Alfred Hitchcock's Jamaica Inn and he took advantage of getting a free haircut from the underused hairdresser he was friendly with. Meanwhile the band continued to play each evening despite them playing to only a handful of passengers on some nights.

One week after leaving Halifax, on the 26th of September, Captain Moulton announced that they had been instructed to divert from Southampton to Plymouth, and then to Dartmouth as their final destination. Jack and the crew were now certain that their ship would be undergoing radical alterations and that they would be discharged at the end of the voyage. As they entered the dangerous western approaches near Ireland they were joined the following day by the destroyer, HMS Amazon, to provide some anti-submarine duties on the final leg. Despite the constant threat of danger, the only injury that had occurred on board was to a Miss Leigh, who when playing paddle tennis on deck in her high heels, slipped, fracturing her left arm!

In fine weather, the convoy split on the 28th of September, with the Arandora Star breaking off to speed up the English Channel, and the three French liners heading to Le Harve, whilst the remainder headed to Liverpool. In the early hours of Friday morning the 29th of September, the Arandora Star reached Plymouth under strict blackout regulations. The passengers disembarked during the morning after their final breakfast on board. Whilst the ship's shop's contents were being packed up, Jack took the opportunity to buy some additional items for presents and keepsakes. After departing early in the afternoon, during the short voyage to Dartmouth the staff in the purser's office completed the final pay slips for the crew and the ship dropped anchor just after 6pm.

All the liners reached their respective ports safely, and having passed the slower convoy HX.1, they became a small piece of history, being the first convoy of the war to reach the UK from North America. Finally anchored in the Dartmouth estuary most of the crew were discharged, as Royal Navy officers boarded to assess the suitability of turning the Arandora Star into an armed merchant cruiser.

With mixed emotions the crew made their way to one of the ship's four launches, which ferried them to the attractive historic town of Dartmouth, nestling in the rolling hills of South Devon. They stepped back onto the quayside with their luggage after almost one month away and passed through customs. Jack shook hands with all his colleagues and wished them luck, hoping to see them soon. He then headed to the phone box at Kingswear Station to ring home.

"Hello, Hull 34472," came the familiar voice of his mother Nora.

"Mum, it's Jack. I've arrived back in the UK, I'm in Dartmouth, Devon."

"Oh Jack, I'm so relieved. I've been so worried since war was declared, and with all the reports of attacks on the shipping."

"I'm fine Mother. I will be staying in Bristol tonight with a friend and should be back home tomorrow afternoon. I'll tell you all about it then."

"That's great Jack. By the way, you're an uncle now. Your sister Joan had a baby girl, Christine, born two weeks ago, so that's another reason to celebrate!"

As Jack headed for the train, eager to see his family again and let them know all about his unexpected adventure, he could not have anticipated that he would never see his colleagues or the Arandora Star again.

'SS Arandora Star, July 1939, cruise in Norway' (author's photographs)

'Deck games on SS Arandora Star, July 1939' (author's photographs)

'Deck games and exercising, SS Arandora Star, July 1939' (author's photographs)

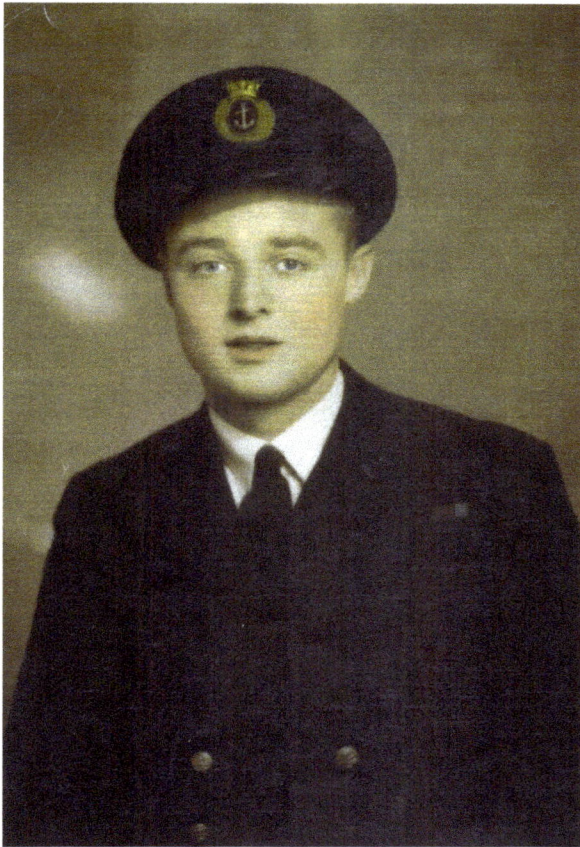

'Jack, March 1939'
(author's photo)

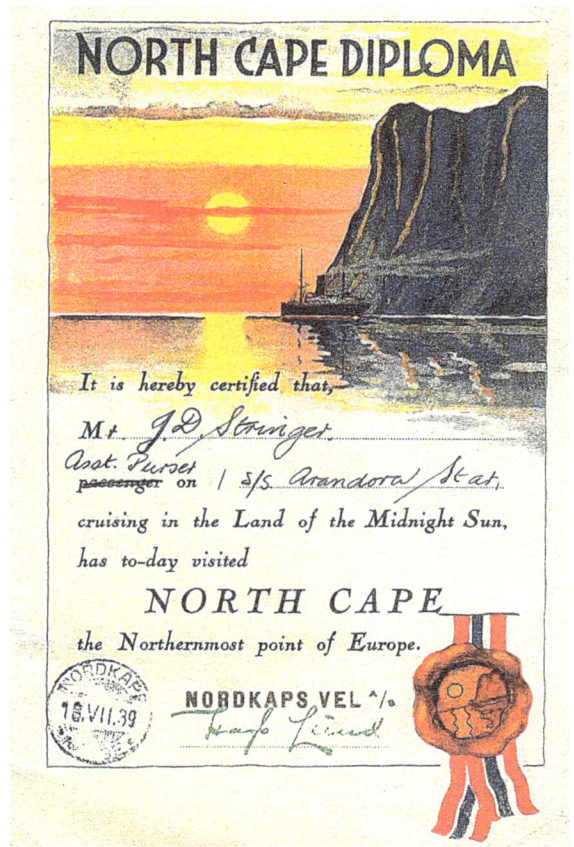

'Jack's "Diploma" 18th July 1939'
(author's photo)

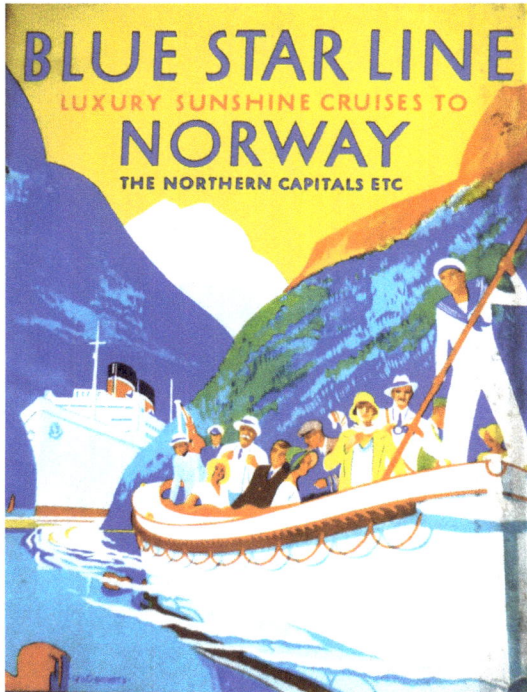

'July 1939, Arandora Star Brochure'
(author's)

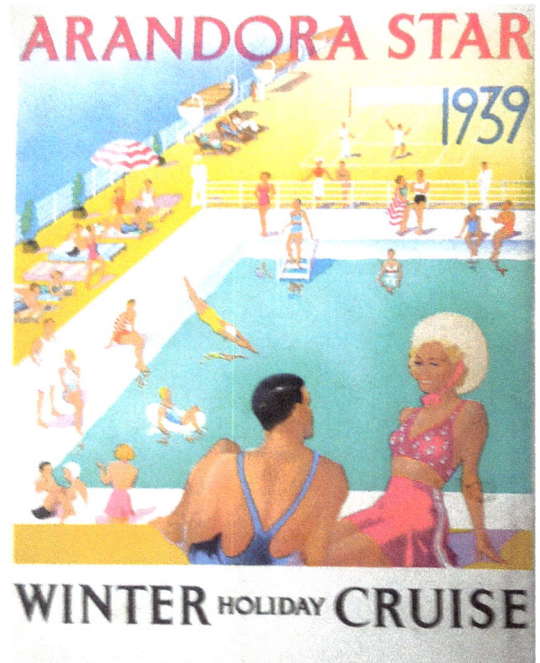

'Cancelled winter cruise brochure for
1939' (author's)

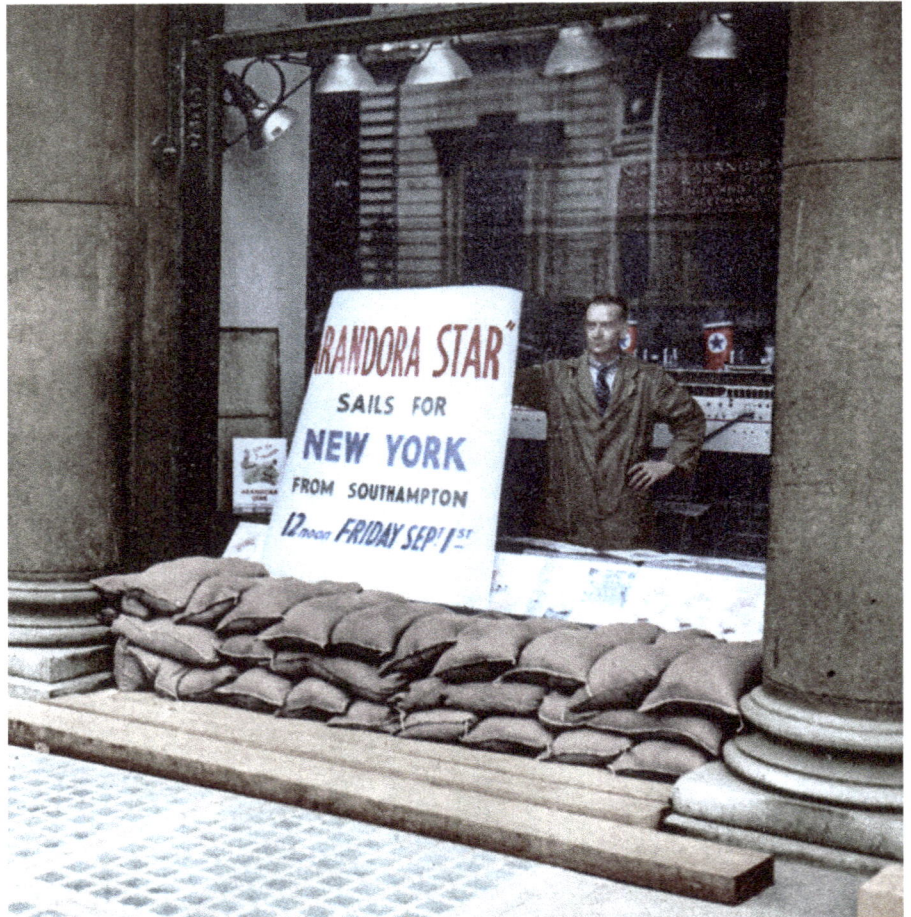

'Blue Star head office,
Regent Street, London,
1st September 1939'
(Illustrated London News,
colour by Grant Kemp)

'Restored original model of SS Arandora Star, now in Science Museum, London.
Visible through the window of the Blue Star office in previous photo'
(author's photo)

'The Montgomery children arriving at New York on board the SS Arandora Star, 12th September 1939' (Everett collection, colour by Grant Kemp)

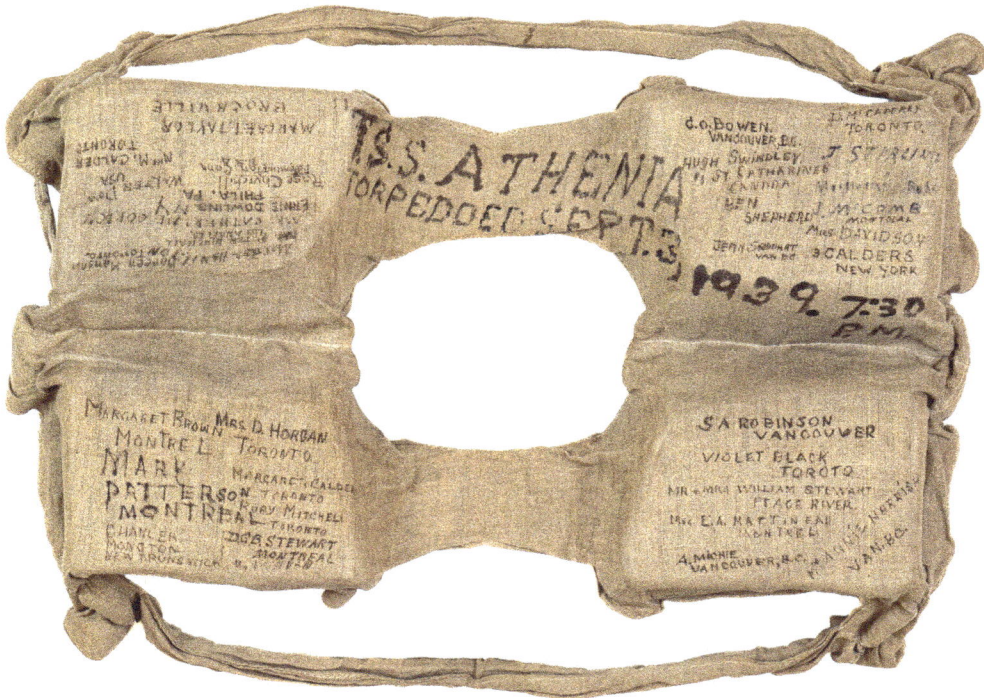

'Lifejacket signed by survivors from one of the lifeboats of the SS Athenia, sunk 3rd September 1939' (WW2 Museum, New Orleans)

Chapter 2
SS Abosso and Radio Training, Hull

It was early Saturday evening on the 23rd of December 1939, almost three months since Jack had arrived home from his eventful voyage on the Arandora Star. The Crown Inn public house on Holderness Road, Hull, was already beginning to fill up, as locals called in on their way back from Christmas shopping in the city centre two miles away. This large popular pub in East Hull, which was built just the year before in a modern art deco style, was also Jack's local, being almost opposite Westcott Street where he lived.

Receiving his change for the two pints he had just bought, he dropped some coins into the large glass jar on the counter which was labelled 'Comfort for the Forces Fund', an organisation that provided help for dependants of enlisted men. The pub's patrons were proud that they had already raised over £70, which was more than any other pub in the city. Heading across the large smoky room which was decorated with Christmas paper chains, wreaths, pinecones and garlands, Jack skirted the practising darts team and groups of chattering locals and reached the wooden table in the corner, where his old school friend Sam Burwell was seated. Sam lived very near to Jack, in Coleridge Street, and had joined the Royal Navy at the outbreak of war. Training to be a gunner in Chatham, Kent, he was due to join the light cruiser HMS Carlisle after Christmas. They had not met up since the previous summer and now they were eager to catch up with each other's news.

Jack explained about his time on the Arandora Star and told Sam that since that adventure he had also been assistant purser on another ship, the SS Abosso, from which he had just returned. The SS Abosso was a modern liner, only four years old but smaller than the Star, with three decks and about 11,000 gross tonnage. Jack had left from Liverpool on the 2nd of November for the ship's usual scheduled run to West Africa. The SS Abosso was carrying mail and 370 passengers, comprising many government officials and civil servants, mining engineers and supervisors, a couple of senior judges, about forty naval personnel, and even a few groups of clergymen and missionaries. Many passengers disembarked in Freetown, Sierra Leone, where the Navy's Fleet Air Arm base was guarding the convoy assembly bay area. The ship then completed her voyage with further stops east along the coast in Takoradi and Accra in Ghana, and finally in Lagos, Nigeria.

However, the Abosso sailed independently the whole time, as it was believed her speed of 14 knots was sufficient to avoid U-Boats. The main worry was the reports of the German pocket battleship Graf Spee, which was twice as fast as the Abosso, and had recently sunk several ships in the South Atlantic. Luckily for Jack, the Graf Spee remained well south of West Africa during his voyage. By the time the Abosso returned to Liverpool on the 9th of December, the Graf Spee had started to head towards South America, and subsequently to her fate.

After swapping stories of their experiences to date, Jack surprised Sam with a newspaper cutting for a new course and career he was starting in the New Year, which read:

THE MERCHANT NAVY
URGENTLY NEED RADIO OFFICERS
Commencing Salary £14 17s 6d per month.
Training Period 6 months. Tuition Fee 4 Guineas.
Age limits 16 to 50. Military Exemption.
Full Particulars from Hull Technical College.

Similar adverts appeared around the country in local papers from November onwards, as there was a serious shortage of around 2,500 Merchant Navy radio officers nationally, and training would now qualify as a reserved occupation. After enjoying another drink and making their arrangements to meet again, the pair headed outside into the cold winter darkness. Jack was going to meet his parents, Leonard and Nora, to go to the Dorchester cinema with them to see the hit film 'Shipyard Sally,' starring Gracie Fields. The Dorchester was one of 36 cinemas in Hull at this time, the peak of popularity for cinema, but by the end of the war this had reduced to 25.

Christmas was a happy and noisy affair in the terraced house at 24 Westcott Street. Jack's older sisters, Gwen and Joan, were there with their partners and Jack's new baby niece. Also present were a couple of seamen from the Hull Seamen's Mission. They had been invited because they were unable to get home during the holiday period, as were more than 100 others. As Joan played the piano in the lounge, with everyone singing along, Leonard and Nora were grateful that at this special time of year the family were able to be together, but they wondered if they would be so lucky in the future. Sam's family also called in to join the festivities, and on Boxing Day the two friends went to a local friendly football match between Hull City and Grimsby Town, held at Anlaby Road, Hull. Although no goals were scored, it was enjoyed by almost six thousand spectators. The two friends said their goodbyes the following day, understanding that as they were seamen they would at high risk of death, in line with the casualty figures just released by the government. These showed that British losses since the start of the war totalled 2,511 (compared to 1,431 French losses), which broke down to 3 men killed on the Western Front, 438 in the Air Force and 2,070 on naval service.

By the end of 1939 the land war in Europe had for the most part not extended beyond Poland, apart from the invasion of southern Finland by the Russians. The Allied and German armies were dug in on their respective borders, and the air war was mainly confined to attacks on local shipping. Since the first day of the war, The Merchant Navy had been subject to attacks, and in the first four months 96 British ships had been sunk.

According to German Admiralty Records there were 57 U-Boats at the outbreak of war, with 49 of all classes available for operational duties, of which 21 of the larger types were stationed in the Atlantic. The British merchant fleet at the outbreak of war was by far the largest in the world with almost 9,000 ships totalling nearly 19 million tons. In addition, there were 2,000 ships of more than 3 million tons in the British Dominions and Colonies. By comparison, the next largest commercial powers were the U.S.A. with over 11 million tons, Japan and Norway each with 4 million tons and Germany with just over 3.6 million tons.

Early in the new year, on Monday the 8th of January 1940, Jack found himself trudging through the sleet in the bitterly freezing wind, as the coldest winter for 45 years moved from mainland Europe to the UK. The polar weather throughout January and February became so severe that the Humber shipping traffic was suspended for three weeks by ice which had formed up to twelve feet thick in places. Jack had planned to cycle the two and a half miles to Park Street just north of the city centre, but due to the weather and blackout restrictions he decided to take the trolley bus, to ensure he arrived on time for his first day at college. Just before 8.30am he walked up the steps of the Hull Municipal Technical College, clutching his bag containing the headphones and books he had purchased the previous week, ready to commence his training as a Radio Officer for the Merchant Navy.

The course Jack was attending, along with more than twenty other young men, was the Postmaster General Special Certificate. This course mainly involved being instructed in transmitting and receiving Morse Telegraphy, and the maintenance of equipment. The usual full course took one year pre-war and led to the qualification of a First Grade Post Office 'Ticket'. The Special Certificate course that Jack was undertaking to become a radio operator had previously been applicable only for use on trawlers. However, with the outbreak of war it became a requirement that 24-hour radio communication cover was necessary, for all but the smallest ships. Consequently, a first, second and third radio officer would become the norm, when previously only one was required. This had therefore immediately resulted in a huge shortage of qualified radio officers. To address this problem classes were set up at about 26 colleges throughout the country, with a view to completing the course to gain a second or third class 'ticket' in around six months.

As Jack sat at his table along with the other students, who ranged in age from 17 to their early 30s, they were informed by a GPO examiner that it would be necessary to send and receive Morse at twenty words per minute in plain language and code, (the first-class requirement was twenty-five words). They would also have to demonstrate an ability to operate and service the heavy-duty marine transistors and receivers, answer questions on wireless theory and learn the many regulations now applying to radio communications.

So began Jack's new career, slowly learning by heart the individual Morse letters, numbers and symbols, represented by dots and dashes, or as they referred to them, 'dits' and 'dahs'. Once they became proficient at these, they would also be learning cyphers which were communicated in figures, and codes which were in letters. A sense of timing would be crucial, to ensure the signals would be spaced correctly, with the eventual aim to send and read without conscious effort.

The basic lessons commenced, with students sitting along both sides of three long wooden tables. One student at the end of each table was to send Morse code messages and all the other students were to listen for a buzzer through their headphones. The sender was instructed to allow the whole of the lower arm to rest comfortably on the table, from the elbow. Holding the knob of the Morse key lightly under the right hand, with the thumb on the left side, the first finger on the top of the front edge and the second finger on the right side, all the sending motion was to be from the wrist. To make a dot or 'dit' the motion was to be as rapid as possible, and a dash or 'dah' was to last three times the length of a dot. The time between two letters was to be equal to three 'dots' and the gap between two words was to be equal to five 'dots'.

By the end of the first day, Jack's head was swimming with information, but he was determined to put in the work to pass the examination. As he headed out of the building into the freezing darkness, other people were already starting to arrive at the college after a full day's work, to attend the various evening courses in building construction. The recent call-up of two million young men between the ages of 20 and 27, for military service, was already starting to add to shortages in many industries and trades.

Over the following months the students gradually improved their understanding and speed of Morse. Jack and the other students had to overcome the wall or plateau in learning that they would invariably reach. This was often around the eight to ten words a minute mark, which seemed impossible to improve on, but it was necessary to progress to reach the required pass rate. To make matters worse, and to add realism to the course, the lecturers would add artificial interferences to replicate poor reception at sea. Through sheer persistence and practice, most of them would finally be able to understand the continuous stream of dots and dashes, hearing it as a form of music, and make the breakthrough to enable them to pass their course.

Most of their time as radio officers was spent listening to messages that they had to report to the captain. As any transmissions offered the enemy opportunities to ascertain their position, strict rules and procedures were in place. These were contained in a thick bound book titled 'Wartime Instructions for Merchant Ships (WIMS) Radio Procedures' which needed to be updated frequently throughout the war. It also included instructions on general security and use of radio equipment (whether in port, in convoy or sailing independently), coding and decoding, call signs, plus details of all the shore-based radio stations transmitting signals to merchant ships throughout the world, known as Broadcast to Allied Merchant Ships (BAMS). However, the regulations regarding sending of distress signals was of prime importance and was studied with even greater attention, as its importance could be a matter of life or death for the crew, with often little time to react.

The components of a distress message for a ship not in convoy would start with the letters CT, meaning attention, then the appropriate distress signal as in the table below.

On the sighting of or being attacked by a warship raider	RRRR RRRR RRRR
an armed merchant ship raider	QQQQ QQQQ QQQQ
a submarine or mine	SSSS SSSS SSSS
an aircraft	AAAA AAAA AAAA
when in immediate danger not due to enemy action, such as an iceberg or collision	SOS SOS SOS

Then the letters DE, followed by:
the war radio call sign of the transmitting ship three times,
then the ship's position,
then the nature of attack,
then the weather report if considered of importance, such as for the benefit of rescue aircraft
    and if time permits,

then the letters AR to show the end of the message.

So, an example of a distress message due to submarine attack would be:

CT (attention) SSSS SSSS SSSS (submarine) DE (from) KRAX KRAX KRAX (ship's unique call sign) 3840 N 7450 W (position Latitude.38-40 degrees North, Longitude.74-50 degrees West) TORPEDOED (nature of attack) AR (end of message). The radio officers would therefore send:

CT SSSS SSSS SSSS DE KRAX KRAX KRAX 3840 N 7450 W TORPEDOED AR

If there was a sighting of a submarine (rather than an attack) the same message would be sent but with the word PERISCOPE instead of TORPEDOED. If a distress signal was sent due to causes unconnected with the enemy a similar message would use the SOS signal and details of the cause such as FIRE IN HOLD OUT OF CONTROL. NEED IMMEDIATE ASSISTANCE.

There were other similar message procedures, for example, where the enemy was trying to jam radio traffic, by using the XXX XXX XXX urgency signal and giving, where possible, a Directional Finding bearing of the enemy's transmitter and strength of the jamming signals.

The primary duty of the radio officer was to monitor the distress messages, which were broadcast on the international calling and distress frequency of 500 kilohertz for Morse code maritime communication. To assist monitoring when there were insufficient radio officers to provide 24-hour coverage, or when they were engaged in another activity, an auto-alarm system was provided which could detect a distress signal and then set off a warning to the radio room via a loudspeaker or alarm bell. Every four hours, on the hour, on long wave (low frequency) which could be received all over the world, radio officers listened for information from Rugby Radio Station and from appropriate area stations, for a list of call signs of all ships there were messages for. The coded messages were then broadcast to the ships in alphabetical order.

Ships in convoy had additional procedures and signalling rules that the students also had to learn. Just before a convoy sailed, the Captain and Senior Radio Officer from each ship would attend a conference organised by the Local Naval Authority. Here, details of routing were disclosed, together with unique call signs for the convoy, the positioning of each ship in a particular convoy and column, details of any escorts, latest weather reports and relevant intelligence reports. A Commodore and Vice Commodore were appointed to be responsible for each convoy, on separate ships, through whom all radio communications were routed. An example of a convoy's call signs when the convoy was assigned the letters 'XY' would be:

Call sign of the main convoy	XYD3
Commodore's call sign	XYD1
Call sign for ships straggling from convoy	XYD9
Call sign of the No.4 column of ships	XYD04
Call sign of ship No.43 (the third ship in the fourth column)	XYD43
Call sign of a section of ships joining convoy	XYS3
Call sign of the Commodore of a joining section	XYS1

Ships in convoy always had to preserve radio silence unless sending a distress message, or if ordered to reply to a call from the Commodore or escort, or to pass on a positive directional finding of the enemy to the Commodore, all in accordance with special instructions received at the convoy conference. There were many other examples of procedures to be learnt, such as signals ordering an alteration of course or speed and how to request a repeat back if the message was not correctly received, which all had to be recorded in the radio log.

Week after week the training continued, and as the freezing winter passed into spring, the war in Europe erupted with the German invasion of Norway and Denmark in April, followed quickly by the conquest of Holland, Belgium, Luxembourg and France by the end of June. With Italy now allied with Germany and Russia, and fascist Spain remaining neutral, Britain was alone in Europe, and her merchant fleet soon became under ever increasing attacks. The Germans' newly acquired bases along the French Atlantic coast meant attacks from their U-Boats and aircraft would now have greater ranges to operate from and be able to push further into the Atlantic. Together with attacks from torpedo boats in the English Channel, and the constant laying of minefields by the Germans near many port estuaries and in the North Sea, British merchant losses quickly escalated.

A foretaste of the devastation which was to come to Hull occurred as Jack and his family slept soundly on Tuesday night the 25th of June. Just after midnight the air raid alarm was sounded. Thinking this was just another false alarm which had occurred for several nights previously, Jack, his sister Gwen and their parents, made their way down to the cupboard under the stairs, which Leonard had rigged up with an electric light and two small benches with cushions. Then suddenly at 1.40am they were wide awake when the nearby anti-aircraft guns burst into life and searchlights scanned the skies. Seconds later several bombs exploded close by, followed by a loud blast very near to them.

Holding on to each other, the family waited anxiously for several minutes for any further explosions, but none came. There was just the barking of several neighbours' dogs, then the ringing of bells from the emergency services vehicles. Just over an hour later the all-clear sounded and fearing the worst, Leonard went outside to see if there was anything they could do to help. Returning after a short while he confirmed that three houses, numbers 130, 132 and 134 had been badly damaged. Several others had windows blown out, and there were numerous holes in nearby roofs, but incredibly no one was seriously injured. Mr. Westerdale from number 134 had had a particularly lucky escape as he was in his neighbour's garden shelter at the time. As they headed off to bed, hoping they could get some sleep before they had to get up for work in a few hours' time, they all realised how fortunate they had been.

The raid affecting Westcott Street was only the second air raid within the city. The very first raid, just five days before, had only caused minor damage to some houses by incendiaries, and some high explosive bombs had damaged a railway bridge parapet in Chamberlain Street, a mile and a half to the north. Sporadic trial and probing raids by the Luftwaffe had begun on the south and east coasts of Britain over the month following the German occupation of Norway, the Low Countries and France. Now, people were starting to realise Britain was facing the full force of the German war machine and it was only a matter of time before the bombers returned in large numbers as the prelude to an invasion.

As Jack returned home that evening, tired from another day of studying at the college, he paused at his front gate to look up the street. It was difficult to reconcile the scene of workmen stretching tarpaulins over damaged roofs, boarding up shattered windows and clearing the broken glass, with other people returning home from their normal working day during the sunniest June on record. Sitting down to tea with his parents and his sister Gwen, the conversation was dominated by the previous night's air raid, and whether they should have had an Anderson shelter in the garden. These had ceased production in March and the last shelters available had been delivered earlier that month, and they all agreed they would be more comfortable staying indoors. Leonard, who was the furnishing manager of the large Co-Op emporium in the city centre, mentioned that to help with any firefighting, the Co-Op were planning to install several large water tanks, hidden under the counters on the top floor, and to protect the staircases with corrugated iron sheets and asbestos. Jack was then given the news that his friend Sam had just returned on leave. After finishing his meal, he walked around the corner to call on him and they both headed down to their nearby local, The Crown, in Holderness Road.

Here Jack learnt that Sam had been heavily involved in the ill-fated landings in the Norway campaign on board HMS Carlisle, an anti-aircraft cruiser. Having landed several thousand troops in central Norway a week after Germany invaded in April, Sam was back there two weeks later in early May, at Namsos near Trondheim, as part of the evacuation convoy.

Listening in awe, Jack heard Sam describe how hellish it had been, stuck in a narrow fjord and constantly under attack from JU87s, Stuka dive bombers. He had only trained for attacks coming in at 45 degrees, but the German pilots dived vertically, straight down at them and his chief gunnery officer was killed almost immediately by the machine guns. They managed to elevate fully and load the eight 4-inch guns, sending up shells every five seconds, maintaining a barrage of 96 rounds per minute. With additional support from smaller guns, they inflicted two definite kills and damaged possibly three more aircraft. The rescue ships managed to get about 6500 men safely away, whilst the rear guard held the Germans at the edge of the town. They were bombed on the way back to Scapa Flow, but luck was with them as the bombs missed them. Sam reported that the army lads all said the whole campaign was a mess from start to finish, with constant changes of where they were to be, with the wrong equipment on the wrong ships, and with no air cover.

This discussion about the war, particularly about the imminent threat of invasion, continued over more drinks and a game of the pub's dominoes, until they headed back home before the blackout came into force, bringing with it the possibility of another air raid. The two nineteen-year-old friends, already more travelled and wiser than most of their contemporaries, shook hands firmly, and wished each other luck in Britain's very uncertain future.

Jack concentrated on his final period of studying over the next few weeks. Suddenly he heard the shocking news that on the morning of the 2nd of July the Arandora Star had been torpedoed and sunk 75 miles off the coast of Northwest Ireland. At this time, the ship had just been instructed to carry over 1,200 Italian and German internees, plus some German P.O.W.s, to Canada for the duration of the war. Over 800 people were lost, the majority being Italian civilians. Captain Moulton, whom Jack had last seen when he left the ship in Dartmouth just over nine months ago, tragically went down with the ship.

Trying to put this disturbing news aside he continued to prepare for his six-hour exam, which finally arrived on Monday the 11th of July. After payment of his £1 examination fee, he was delighted to hear that he had passed his practical and written tests and gained his Postmaster General Special Certificate of Proficiency in Radiotelegraphy.

However, a frustrating waiting period unexpectedly followed. Having enrolled into the Merchant Navy Reserve, where his name would be forwarded to operating companies and ship owners who wished to take on radio officers, nothing further was heard. Finally in mid-August he was contacted by Marconi International Marine Company to attend at the local office at 30 Albion Street in Hull city centre. On arrival, he signed and filled in various forms, giving his personal details, and he was then sent for a medical. Being passed physically fit, Jack preceded to order a new double-breasted jacket, trousers and hat, with the appropriate wireless officer insignias, from Kenneth and Bradley Tailors.

Reporting at the Marconi office each day over the next couple of weeks, along with a few of his classmates, Jack became increasingly disappointed with the delay when his name was not called by the clerk behind the counter to allocate him a position on a ship. To relieve the boredom, the group of former fellow students played numerous games of cards, read shared magazines and newspapers, and practised their Morse skills with one another. This was interspersed with listening to returning seamen receiving their new orders and travel warrants. However, very rarely would these returning seamen share their often-horrendous experiences to the group of fresh-faced young men staring at them and asking them questions.

This unexpected delay was largely due to a re-organisation, with decisions to be made about where the rapid increase in students would be allocated. The numbers of radio students had increased from 1,640 when Jack started at the beginning of the year, to 2,500 in March and then over 4,000 by May. There were also difficulties with getting enough increased accommodation on ships to allow for three radio officers, in contrast to the one radio officer needed pre-war, because unions wanted separate cabins for each officer. Crucially at this time, the RAF urgently required 1,500 more wireless officers, so it was decided that anyone who was 20 - 27 years old on the 1st of July, who had gained their certificate, would join the RAF rather than joining the Merchant Navy. In August, this led to protests in some colleges, including Hull, especially as reimbursement of fees would be considerably lower than the cost incurred by the students. Jack therefore came very close in terms of age to being redeployed to the RAF, only missing it by a matter of weeks as he would not be 20 years old until August.

Most weeks, Jack and his father Leonard would find time to wander down to the Humber docks areas to observe from a distance the ships entering or leaving. The waterborne barges were still operating their barrage balloons, despite some unsuccessful recent nighttime air raids on the docks. These defences were part of 74 barrage balloons that were located throughout the city, although there was one fewer when on the 15th of August, just at the end of his street, the barrage balloon flying above the tennis courts in East Park was shot down in flames. A passing Juncker 88 bomber, which had been part of a group of 50 planes which had attacked RAF Driffield in North Yorkshire, fired its parting shots before returning to its base in Denmark.

The seemingly endless days of unusually dry and fine weather of August provided the perfect backdrop for the Battle of Britain now taking place in the sky above and on the shipping in the coastal waters. Each night at 9pm the latest details were listened to with eager anticipation by Jack, his family, and the whole country, as they tuned in to the BBC News on the radio. The unexpected wait for Jack did at least enable him to celebrate his eldest sister Gwen getting married at the local church, St. Columba's, on the 19th of August. He then enjoyed his own 20th birthday the following week, despite increasing sporadic air raids, including the first fatalities in the city following a hit on an Anderson shelter in Rustenburg Street, just half a mile away. Finally, on Friday the 6th of September Jack was informed that he had been assigned to the ship that he was to serve on as second radio officer, the SS Heminge. On Tuesday the 10th of September, he had to report for duty at South Shields on the River Tyne, 10 miles downstream from Newcastle.

Early on that Tuesday morning, Jack finished putting the last of his belongings into his two leather suitcases. He was glad that his mother had received news the previous night that his elder sister Joan had just given birth to a healthy son, Tony. Jack hoped that this new arrival of a grandson for Nora would help keep her mind from worrying about him too much. Saying his farewells, he left the house and set off for Paragon Railway Station in the city centre, with his travel warrant to travel north. He felt a mixture of excitement and nervous energy, wondering if he would get to see his new nephew by Christmas.

'Sam Burwell (left) and Jack, 26th December 1939, Queen Victoria Square, Hull'
(author's photo, colour Grant Kemp)

'The newly built Crown Pub, Holderness Road, Hull, 1939'
(photo from Nicky Guest-Walmsley, colour Grant Kemp)

'134 and 136 Westcott Street, Hull, bomb damage, 26ᵗʰ June 1940'
(Hull Daily Mail, Mirrorpix, colour Grant Kemp)

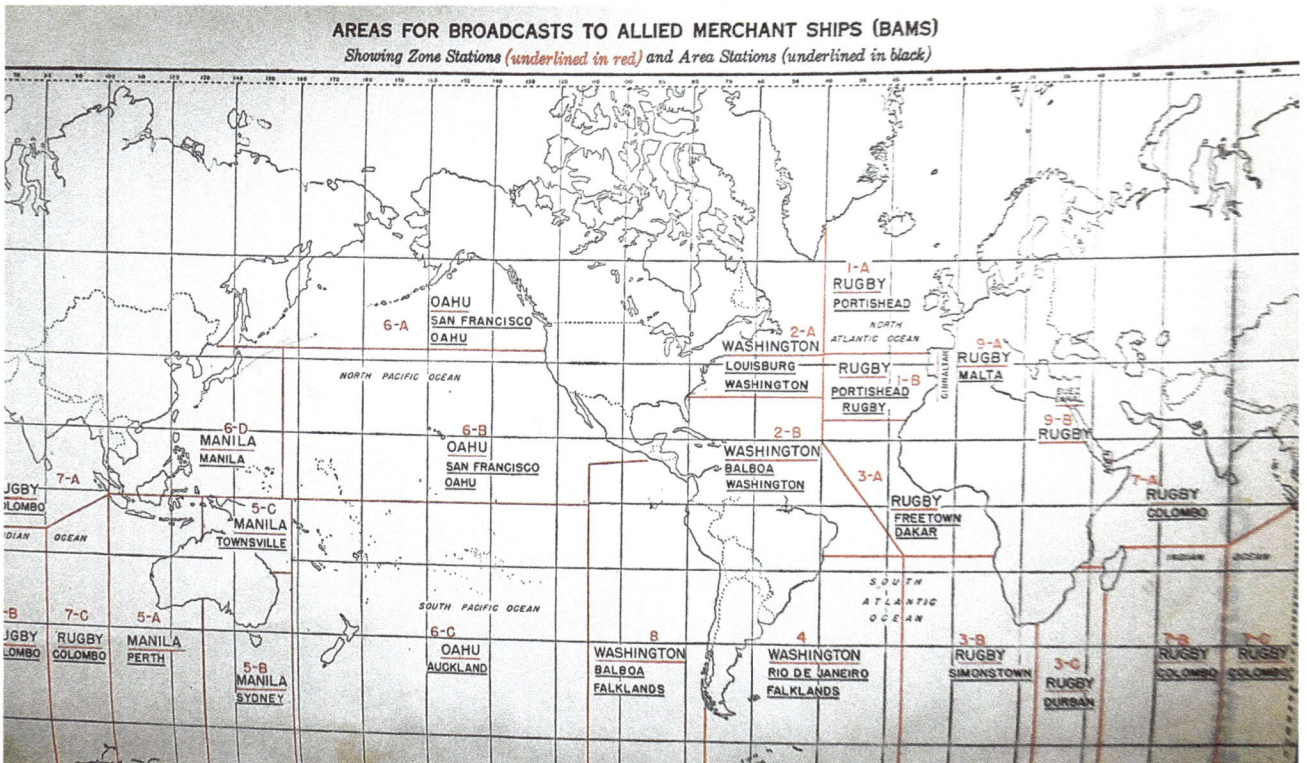

'Map from Admiralty WIMS book' (Author's)

elephone : HEADQUARTERS 1234.

elegrams : Gentel Cent London

Any reply should be addressed to
THE INSPECTOR OF WIRELESS TELEGRAPHY.

TELECOMMUNICATIONS DEPARTMENT,
GENERAL POST OFFICE,
LONDON, E.C.I.

ur Reference   P.O. Reference

Dear Sir,

The question of the supply of Wireless Operators for the Merchant Navy and the Royal Air Force has again been under review.

It has been decided that all men registered under the National Service (Armed Forces) Act who were born between 1913 and 1920, both years inclusive, will, on obtaining the Special Certificate, be enlisted into the Signals Branch of the Royal Air Force under the conditions specified in enclosure A to my letter of 1st July, 1940.

Men of all other ages will, on obtaining the Special Certificate, be available for employment in the Merchant Navy, where there are now vacancies, but may volunteer for the Royal Air Force or other branches of the Armed Forces. Men of 35 and upwards may continue to volunteer for employment as Civilian W.T. Operators at Royal Air Force stations.

The above arrangements are subject to revision from time to time to meet the varying needs of the Merchant Navy and the Armed Forces.

Please post a copy of this letter in your School for the information of the Students.

Yours faithfully,

C.E.Brawley.

Inspector of Wireless Telegraphy.

To Principals of Marine Schools.

'5th August 1940 notification of change of rules for new radio officers wishing to join the Merchant Navy, to join the R.A.F. instead - which Jack just avoided' (Kew National Archives)

Chapter 3
SS Heminge

Having signed on at the South Shields shipping office and been pointed in the right direction, Jack lugged his suitcases through the busy dock area and past numerous rail trucks which were piled high with coal from the nearby coalfields. He headed to the blackened wooden decking of the Harton Staithes (wharves), where he saw his ship which was moored alongside. Built locally in Hartlepool in 1919, the SS Heminge was a 2,500 ton tramp steamer now owned by the shipping company Constants, who had a small fleet of ten vessels all named after Kent villages. Since its launch, the Heminge had been in continual service, usually carrying 3,500 tons of coal from her home port of Newcastle, or from South Wales where Constants had an office, to the Mediterranean, then returning with iron ore. Like thousands of other similar vessels, they were the workhorses of the British Merchant Navy, but were used to their capacity, as shipping owners extracted the maximum return from them, whilst spending as little as possible on either the ships or the crews.

As Jack cast his eyes over the grey metal plates streaked with rust, his new home seemed to merge perfectly with the dark black water of the River Tyne, compounded by the flotsam of this industrial river which was collecting alongside the hull and wharf. His gaze was soon diverted by a loud crash which continued for several seconds, as another load fell into the ship's hold from the chute above, followed by a billowing dark cloud of dust, confirming the nature of their cargo to be coal. Already beginning to taste the black particles, he nervously made his way up the gangway as the rattle of the coal subsided. The racket was replaced by the shouts and swearing of the ship's trimmers hidden in the cargo holds, who were trying to ensure that they spread 3,500 tons of coal evenly with their shovels.

Jack stood on the deck, looked around at several of his new companions who all appeared suntanned and weathered from years at sea, and wondered if he might be the youngest on board. Breathing in the smell of fresh tar which was being applied to the joints of a section of wooden decking that was being replaced and hearing the banging of hammers on metal below deck, he wondered where he should go. Then a man with a strong Welsh accent introduced himself as Alan Owen, an experienced steward. Alan proceeded to guide Jack to his cabin off a small corridor amidships, between the two cargo holds. This room could not have been more unlike his accommodation on previous cruise liners, but it was even worse than he expected. It was cramped, just long enough for a single bed with a cupboard next to it, with a cracked sink and matching small, cracked mirror above. The nicotine stains on the ceiling were gradually covering the faded cream paintwork and dead insects seemed to litter the floor, mixed with a thin layer of coal dust. Alan advised Jack to leave his suitcases there and head up to the radio room to meet the first radio officer, while he organised some help to clean the cabin, as the coal loading was almost complete.

The radio room was easy to locate being where the radio aerial descended from the top of the mast. To help to protect the room, it was surrounded by concrete blocks with sandbags on top. Inside, Jack was surprised to be greeted by a young man of similar age to himself. He was from Shropshire, had a Greek heritage, and was named Theo. They immediately struck up a bond despite Theo's seniority. Jack spent the next couple of hours becoming familiar with the equipment, practising sending messages on a dead Morse key, then listening to and recording messages with the receiver turned on to 600 metres. Pleased with his efforts Jack went back to his cabin where he met the youngest and most junior member of the crew, Charlie, the 16-year-old Mess Room Boy. Between them they scrubbed and cleaned the room and added some new bedding provided by the Steward. Jack was also provided with a life jacket with the advice to keep it close at hand, or to sleep in it at night when at sea in known danger areas. The final piece of advice was not to forget to wedge the door open when sleeping, to avoid it jamming, which could lead to Jack becoming trapped if the ship was hit. As Jack unpacked, the realisation of what he had signed up to took hold.

The evening meal in the saloon provided Jack with the chance to meet the experienced Captain Trevor Thomas. He was 39 years old, from Cardiff and regarded as firm but fair by his crew. Jack also met five other officers, most of whom were also from Wales. In contrast to several horror stories which Jack had heard about the poor quality of food on board merchant ships, his hunger was satisfied with the meal. First there was soup, then cold meat, peas and potatoes, followed by a sweet called plum duff, which was a dough mixture enhanced with whatever the cook wanted to get rid of, hidden beneath thick custard, and finally coffee. The Captain then informed them that as all loading was complete, they would soon be moving a mile downriver, to just outside the mouth of the Tyne, where they would await instructions to join a convoy.

The following day Jack spent his time helping Theo with maintenance duties, including replacing the old heavy batteries with the new ones that had just arrived, and checking all the equipment and the aerial. Then he had to read the related manuals, to become fully accustomed with the operation of everything he would be using. This time at anchor allowed him to get acquainted with the rest of the crew, which totalled 26, and like in most of the Merchant Navy there was a mixture of nationalities to maintain its vast fleet. Two seamen were from Denmark and Holland and had been at sea when their countries were recently invaded; one man was from Canada; and the six firemen and trimmers who kept the boilers fed were from Celyon, Jamaica and Somalia.

The remaining crew were from around Britain, including one gunner assigned to the ship, a middle-aged reservist Royal Marine from Kent, who along with almost half the crew had joined the ship around the same time as Jack. He took great delight in showing the workings of the 4-inch gun mounted on the stern to anyone who showed an interest. This gun was intended for use against submarines and had been in storage for twenty years since the end of the last war. The other armaments consisted of two light machine guns on the bridge, a Lewis and a Hotchkiss, neither of which were particularly effective against aircraft. The more powerful Oerlikons and Bofors machine guns were not available at the time, due to there being insufficient numbers. Several of the crew had been on a two-day course, first implemented in 1938, to operate and maintain these machine guns, which also gave them a slight increase in their pay. The aim was to have 5,500 merchant ships defensively armed but so far only around half had been completed. The intention to have several fully qualified army and naval trained gunners on each ship was a long way from happening, especially with the threat of imminent invasion.

Following his return from a visit to shore, the Captain informed the officers they had orders to depart, along with two other ships moored near them. They were to join one of the regular convoys which had been in operation since the start of the war. They were going to head north to join the convoy which was coming from Southend and the Thames and then travel together to Methil on the River Forth, Scotland. From Methil they would join convoys heading around the north of Scotland and Northern Ireland, going into the North Atlantic before heading south independently to their destination, Tenerife in the Canary Islands.

With just the two radio officers on board, and under orders to keep a continuous radio watch, Jack was assigned the midnight to 6am and midday to 6pm shifts. Just after midnight the ship headed down the river. Theo made sure Jack felt confident about decoding any incoming messages, and was aware of the list of call signs for the 23 other ships in the convoy they were joining. He also informed Jack to only notify the Captain of distress calls from other ships if they were close to their position, as he would probably hear many distress calls during their voyage. Finally, Theo reminded Jack to dispose of the radio log, coding and decoding books by placing them into the weighted canvas bag before throwing them overboard in the event of receiving orders of having to abandon the ship.

On entering the North Sea, the Heminge joined the rear of the convoy heading north, and Jack felt the familiar roll of a ship in the open waters. Although he knew they would be only about two miles offshore along this east coast leg of the voyage, it required enormous concentration to follow a fixed swept channel which was only a few hundred yards wide and marked by light buoys every five miles, especially in the pitch dark and poor weather conditions. To the east of their course lay a huge minefield of several miles in width, which had recently been completed, stretching from Essex to the Orkneys to deter enemy submarines, motor torpedo craft and potential invasion craft. The risk from mines detaching, plus minelaying by German ships, submarines and aircraft, added more risks to the convoys, but confined to his small stuffy room Jack's main concern was keeping awake until the end of his watch. The split shift system meant it was difficult to get adequate sleep, but at least on this first short voyage his watch ended early when they arrived off Methil at 3.30am on the 13th of September, in darkness. Methil was an important coal port, and up until the start of the war had been a herring fishing port, situated on the north side of the Forth estuary. Here a new convoy would form to take them outward-bound to the Atlantic, with a new convoy number OA.214.

Later that day, as the ship lay at anchor, Jack was carrying out the daily check on the batteries when he was called to the bridge. The men on watch were excited to get a close-up view through their binoculars, of a naval task force arriving from the Home Fleet based at Scapa Flow in the Orkney Islands. They were heading along the main channel near the north shore close to their convoy, to the naval port of Rosyth 20 miles up-river. To cheers from crews, and blasts from the merchant ships' horns, they watched the battleships HMS Nelson and HMS Rodney, the battlecruiser HMS Hood, plus three cruisers and seven destroyers steam past, as they were being urgently redeployed to Rosyth to be nearer potential invasion sites in England.

Jack and the rest of the crew remained on board in the sheltered waters known as Methil Roads, and unless provisions were required only the captains were to go ashore, to attend the convoy conference. This was held in the old Miners' Institute building close to the docks, which was known during the war as HMS Sentinel, and was the local naval headquarters for this important convoy formation area. Their convoy would comprise 26 ships and two small naval escorts to provide limited anti-submarine and rescue duties. Once routing instructions, codes, intelligence and weather reports had been provided, plus the appointment of the convoy commander and vice commander made, the Heminge departed with the rest of the convoy just after sunrise the following day, Saturday morning, the 14th of September.

Unfortunately, problems occurred almost immediately, as within two hours of leaving Methil and the estuary's defensive minefields, once in the North Sea the Heminge had fallen behind the rest of the convoy and began to lose sight of them. One of the escorts raced back to see what the problem was, but due to lack of steam pressure the Heminge was unable to keep pace. The Heminge's Captain was advised to continue with the agreed routing instructions until the problem was fixed or put into a port.

Throughout the next three days, the Captain became increasingly frustrated with what he perceived as the inefficiency of the stokehold crew. He believed they were not fit for purpose physically or mentally, and to make matters worse two of them reported sick and refused to continue to work. He asked the engineers and one of the deck crew to help when possible, but to no avail. By the time they had reached the most northerly point of Northern Ireland he realised he would not be able to rejoin the convoy and had no choice but to put into the Clyde to find replacement crew.

Luckily there had only been one aircraft attack on an Allied ship along their route which was the SS Nailsea River, sailing south of them off East Montrose. The weather had been generally good with only partial cloud. Jack and the rest of the crew felt relieved once they reached the safety of the Clyde on the morning of the 18th of September. They had been feeling the strain of being on constant alert and believed they were particularly vulnerable on a ship which was alone and only averaging five or six knots. Although they now felt secure from U-Boat attack, just six hours before their arrival Jack had heard the radio warnings, which were passed to the Captain, regarding an air attack in Glasgow. This turned out to be a lone German bomber which had attacked and scored a direct hit on the cruiser H.M.S. Sussex, which was berthed at Yorkhill Quay, 25 miles upriver in Glasgow, causing it extensive damage with fires lasting for more than 12 hours.

At the time the Heminge arrived in the Firth of Clyde a huge logistical shipping operation was taking shape. This stretch of protected water lay behind the one-and-a-half-mile anti-submarine steel net defence boom, which stretched from Dunoon on the west bank of the Firth of Clyde to the Cloch lighthouse on the east bank. It had become clear during the year that additional safe-port areas would be required to sustain the war effort. Plans to create the Clyde Anchorage Emergency Port were put into effect immediately after the start of the blitz when the London docks were attacked on the 7th of September. This involved creating a dock on the water where ocean-going ships could load and discharge cargoes directly over their sides to smaller coasters, rather than onto quays and into sheds, thus saving valuable time and spreading any risks among many more ships. In addition, hundreds of dock workers, together with their powered or towed flat barges, electric cranes and trucks, were transferred from London, which also allowed certain cargoes to be forwarded by rail or road. Within one week the first cargo ship was unloaded from this anchorage, just four days before the Heminge arrived to witness the beginning of this huge undertaking.

While the engineers on the Heminge worked on the boilers to try to improve their efficiency, the crew spent a frustrating week stuck on board. The Heminge was lying at anchor awaiting the new firemen and trimmers, and details of the next convoy. After one week, six new crew members were signed on from West Africa, Barbados and Mauritius. Finally, two days later, on the 27th of September, just after sunset at 19.30, the Heminge steamed out from the safety of the Clyde. There she joined the tail end of convoy OB.220 which was one of a series of convoys leaving from Liverpool and heading to the Americas. This convoy consisted of 35 merchant ships, and five escorts who would remain with them for the first three days. The Heminge would remain in the convoy until the dispersal area around 400 miles west of Ireland. It would then proceed independently to Tenerife, where the crew were looking forward to some warmer weather as an alternative to the now increasingly cooler autumnal temperatures, with mists and dull skies around northern Britain. Continuing the same watch hours as previously, Jack was aware that the most dangerous period of their voyage was approaching, entering the Atlantic around Northern Ireland. This area was nicknamed U-Boat alley, as it was a favoured area for the enemy to attack, so distress calls, submarine positions and warnings were now frequently being picked up in the radio room.

For two days the Heminge kept up with the convoy, but then it slowly started to drop astern. When the Heminge was four miles adrift, one of the escorts, H.M.S. Wellington, sped back and signalled to close up before dark, or if unable to do so, to alter course in the morning to the agreed rendezvous. Unable to catch up, they carried on by themselves throughout the night, altered course in the morning as agreed, and zigzagged as a precaution, but even with maximum effort they could not make more than eight knots, still just below the convoy's speed. On reaching the rendezvous, the seas were still disappointingly empty, so the Captain decided he had no choice but to continue the voyage independently. Just before sunset there was a cry from the bridge look-out, as something was spotted in the water ahead. Jack rushed from the saloon out onto the deck, along with some of the other officers, who were awaiting their evening meal. They soon came up to a lifeboat, but it was waterlogged, no one was in it, and there were no visible markings to identify it.

The evening meal involved a discussion of the possible origin of the lifeboat, using information from the earlier radio reports of ships recently attacked in the area and the effects of tides and prevailing winds, which were now getting stronger. Jack did not stay long as he needed to get some sleep before the start of his next watch at midnight, so he left after the Captain, who also wanted a brief rest. Neither would get the sleep they expected.

At 21.10 hours on the 30th of September 1940, 420 miles west of Ireland, there was a sudden loud but dull explosion right underneath the Captain's cabin. A torpedo had struck the ship on the starboard side abreast of the bridge. It passed into the bunkers, through the bunker bulkhead and into the after part of number two hold. The bottom of the cabin was blown out and there was a huge eruption of water on both sides of the ship. The deck on both sides amidships was opened up, water poured down inside the ship, with smoke quickly filling the engine room and the Captain's cabin, after the bridge was wrecked and collapsed on top of it. The Captain found himself trapped but luckily, he managed to find the axe he kept in there and broke down the blocked door to find the lights had all gone off in the ship. He tried to find his way to the wireless room, and he was searching for the first mate who had been in command at the time. On this very dark night the confusion was made even worse by a continuous ear-piercing whistle. Some of the debris had fallen onto the whistle lanyard, causing the whistle to blow continuously at full blast, making it impossible to issue orders or for anyone to even hear themselves speak.

Finally reaching the wireless room to make sure a distress signal was sent, the Captain met Theo the chief radio officer. As flames and dense smoke poured out of the room, Theo managed to shout out, between coughing fits, that no SOS signal could be sent, as the wireless and batteries were wrecked. Trying to get further damage information from the other officers, the Captain heard from the chief engineer that he had shut the throttle of the engines when water had poured in, and the dynamo was destroyed. On realising the ship was now listing to starboard and going down by the head, and feeling fearful of another torpedo strike, the Captain managed to issue instructions, shouting to be heard above the nerve-wrecking din from the steam whistle. All crew were to muster by the port side lifeboat, as the starboard boat was missing having been smashed by the explosion.

At the moment of the explosion Jack was asleep in his pyjamas in his cabin, and in those first few moments he was unable to comprehend the noises and shuddering movements in the ship, quickly followed by the siren alarm, loud crashes and shouting around him. Jack quickly located his lifejacket which was on his bed and put it on. He somehow shoved his feet into his shoes in the darkness and stumbled out to the corridor, thankful that he had left his door ajar as advised when he first joined the ship. Hearing shouts of "we've been hit, get on deck", he caught glimpses of people heading outside. Thinking he needed to head to the radio room, he started to hurry toward it, passing number two hold. Suddenly he tripped on an upturned metal plate and felt himself falling headfirst, before hitting the cargo of coal several feet below. Briefly losing consciousness, and feeling cuts on his body and head, he tried to scramble upright but couldn't get enough purchase because the coal kept sliding as the ship started to tilt. Still not aware fully of what had happened, and fearing being trapped in this pitch-black darkness, suddenly a hand grabbed the top of his lifejacket and pulled him to the side of the hold. Amid shouts over the incessant high-pitched steam whistle, he was dragged onto the deck and pushed along in a daze towards the group of figures by the remaining lifeboat.

The rest of the crew gradually assembled for a rough muster in the darkness by the port lifeboat. It was discovered that the after fall was missing, leaving only six inches of rope. Although the starboard lifeboat had been destroyed by the explosion, its fall was discovered on the ship's deck. This was fastened tightly to the insufficient port lifeboat's rope, so that eventually the port boat could be lowered on this single rope. Much to everyone's relief, this was successful, without it getting damaged or disappearing into the sea swell. Finally, after everyone had climbed down the rope ladder safely and been counted, it was discovered that one of the firemen was missing. He had been in the stokehold when the explosion occurred, water had rushed into the engine room, and he had not been seen since. The Captain ordered the oarsmen to pull away fast as the ship suddenly lurched violently. Accompanied by the sound of screeching metal plates, the ship was listing heavily with the bows almost underwater, although it still somehow managed to stay afloat.

As the crew huddled together, the lifeboat gradually pulled away astern, and soon it was impossible to see even the outline of the ship, only a flame was visible coming out of the sea. There now appeared to be flashing lights in the area, which initially the Captain was going to answer, but on second thoughts he decided not to. He realised in time that this was more likely to be the enemy submarine now on the surface, rather than a friendly ship. He ordered the crew to keep as low as possible and not to smoke. They spent the next hour dodging the bright flashes from three or four strong lamps coming from the conning tower of the submarine, which flickered across the sea, as the enemy hoped to track down the survivors to ascertain the ship's name and take the Captain prisoner. Not wanting to light up the oil lamp for the lifeboat's compass, they were pulling in circles, but eventually the flames from the ship disappeared as it sunk. The lights from the submarine also finally ceased, so the sail was hoisted, and they set off towards the east and the coast of Ireland.

Jack was now feeling the cold, shivering continually despite someone sharing a blanket with him, and the painful cuts to his body were aggravated by the saltwater spray splashing over them. To help with the cold everyone was allowed a swig of brandy which had been thoughtfully stored in the lifeboat, along with emergency rations of biscuits and containers of water. For the next five hours the crew huddled together to try and preserve some warmth whilst the Captain and the first mate took it in turns to keep the boat on course. With no sleep possible as they travelled through the waves, the exhausted crew barely talked unless in response to the requests to help bail out any sea water.

At 02.45 hours on the 1st of October an observant sailor on the modern freighter SS Clan Cumming, bound from Australia to Liverpool, spotted a small flickering light coming from a boat in the distance. He informed his Captain, who directed his ship to pull alongside to investigate. Jack and the rest of the crew were jubilant as their Captain Thomas called up to the crew who were looking over from the side of the rescue ship, to say that they were from the sunken cargo ship the Heminge. Within 15 minutes they had all safely boarded the freighter and were on their way. Taken below, into the warmth of the ship, Jack was extremely grateful to be given an old brown suit to wear from one of the Clan's crew, as he had lost everything. After having any wounds attended to, they all appreciated the hospitality given to them including the hot drinks, an early breakfast and a bunk to sleep in. Three days later they had safely arrived in Liverpool, and although this vital port was beginning to be targeted by enemy bombers, fortunately none appeared that day. However, the following week the Luftwaffe bombed Liverpool Harbour, and the Clan Cumming suffered damage, along with three other ships, and one member of its crew died.

Having picked up a travel warrant and a small wage advance from the Marconi office, worried that his parents would have heard about his ship being sunk, Jack phoned his mother to say he was on his way home by train and should be in Hull that evening. When Jack arrived at Paragon Station in Hull in the evening, his parents and his sister Gwen barely recognised him. As he walked towards them in the ill-fitting suit, they could see that he had changed greatly from the smart young man in uniform whom they had last seen just three weeks previously. For many days, Jack was reluctant to talk about his experience. Even when he did speak about what had happened, he just gave the barest of details, like most men returning from similar voyages who were just thankful to be alive.

The unfortunate man who died in the stokehold in the bowels of the ship was 44-year-old John Davies, who had lived on Greenwood Avenue, North Hull. He was one of the replacement firemen taken on in Glasgow after the dismissal of the original stokers, just five days before the ship was hit. Jack and the rest of the crew of the Heminge knew they had been extremely fortunate to survive in the life and death lottery of the Atlantic convoys. Earlier on the same day, the 30th of September, the British cargo ship Samala was torpedoed about 30 miles away from the Heminge, with the loss of all 68 of its crew. This attack was carried out by the same submarine, U-37, which was commanded by 33-year-old Victor Oehrn. This submarine subsequently returned to the newly acquired port of Lorient in Brittany, France. Within the space of just 16 days this U-Boat had sunk a total of six merchant ships with just 105 crew surviving, from a combined complement of 255 men.

'Collier ship loading coal at Harton Coal Staithes, South Shields, April 1939.
This is where Jack joined the Heminge five months later.'
(Amy Flagg, South Tyneside Museum, colour by Grant Kemp)

'SS Heminge' (Paul Johnson collection)

'Methil Miners' Institute building, 2024. Local naval headquarters during the war, was known as HMS Sentinel' (Author's photo)

'Surrendered German merchant vessels where Allied convoys once gathered, Methil, 1945' (I.W.M.)

REGISTERED OFFICE: MARCONI OFFICES, ELECTRA HOUSE.
VICTORIA EMBANKMENT, LONDON, W.C.2.
TELEGRAMS: THULIUM, ESTRAND, LONDON.
TELEPHONE: TEMPLE BAR 4321 (PRIVATE BRANCH EX)

The Marconi International Marine Communication Company, Limited

Marconi House, Chelmsford.

TELEPHONE: CHELMSFORD 3141
TELEGRAMS: THULIUM CHELMSFORD
CODES: MARCONI INTERNATIONAL, ETC

PLEASE ADDRESS THE COMPANY AND
REFER TO   S/1 /Operatin

10th October, 1940.

Mr. J. D. Stringer,
24 Westcott Street,
Hull.

Dear Sir,

We have learned with much regret, of the recent
loss by enemy action, of the vessel on which you were
serving in the capacity of radio officer.

We were very pleased, nevertheless, to receive news
of your subsequent safe arrival in this country, and we
are particularly gratified to know that you escaped
physical injury.

At the same time, we realise that, as a result of
this ordeal, a period of recuperation is necessary, and
we therefore trust you are taking full advantage of the
leave of absence which has been granted to you and that
you will eventually return to duty none the worse for
such a trying experience.

In conclusion, we would express the earnest hope
that in the future you and the ships you sail in will
meet with nothing but good fortune.

Yours faithfully,
THE MARCONI INTERNATIONAL MARINE
COMMUNICATION COMPANY LIMITED

ASSISTANT GENERAL MANAGER (OPERATING AND TRAFFIC)

'Marconi letter dated 10th October 1940, regarding Jack's first sinking' (author's)

Chapter 4
SS Urla

The ordeal of the sinking of the Heminge was a harsh reminder of the horrors of war which from time to time would surface in nightmares for Jack long after the end of the war. His parents tried their best to alleviate his mood during his leave period of three weeks, which included an additional seven days granted by his employer Marconi due to the sinking. Having a visit from his eldest sister Joan with her newly born son and young daughter was a welcome distraction, but it was not long before he had to think about his next voyage. He had to purchase items to replace the clothing and items he had lost, as no compensation was provided. Although Jack would continue to receive his wages from Marconi, the additional war risk payment which had increased to £5 per month, ceased on the date a ship sunk until the member of crew was re-employed. For most of the rest of the crew the lack of wages was even worse as the shipping companies stopped all their wages on the date a ship sunk, no matter how long it took to get back and sign on again. This appalling money saving scheme was finally overturned in May 1941 by the government. This was one of the reasons some Merchant Navy crew personnel wore their small metal lapel badges with the letters MN upside down, showing NW, meaning not wanted.

However, the journey to Jack's new ship was a mere two miles, as it was situated at the Victoria Docks in Hull, one of the city's six docks, which predominantly handled timber cargoes. His trepidation was not improved by seeing his latest vessel, the SS Urla, another old tired-looking tramp steamer built in 1924 in Ardrossan, of 5,200 tons. The crew would number forty-one, plus 35-year-old Captain Marsden from South Wales. They were all British, except the young third mate from Ecuador, and around half of the men had signed on the ship in Hull on the 23rd of September. The officers had all been on the ship on its last voyage which was to Canada to pick up timber, and the feeling was that this trip would be the same, which turned out to be true. Jack's chief radio officer was 32-year-old David Bissett from Scotland, who took Jack under his wing after learning of his recent escape, and they developed a good working relationship.

All the crew were acutely aware of the dangers they were facing as recent losses to British and Allied shipping from the German U-Boats had dramatically increased over the course of the summer and into the autumn. This was due to several factors: the full use of the French ports saving valuable time to reach the Atlantic, acquiring French airfields for long range reconnaissance and bombing, the lack of British naval escorts, the loss of the French fleet, and the deciphering of the British Naval Cypher No.3 which allowed the Germans to estimate Allied convoy movements and timings. At this time, the beginning of U-Boats hunting in small groups was being developed successfully by a small number of experienced commanders, which would develop into wolfpacks of larger numbers of submarines attacking together the following year.

Adding to this pressure, in September Italian submarines started arriving at Bordeaux for use in the Atlantic, and powerful German battlecruisers begun to roam the ocean to cause more panic. Threats from Norway to the Spanish border now faced British and Allied shipping. As the Urla departed Hull docks in ballast on the 25th of October due for Canada, Jack was sadly updating the radio room's list of merchant shipping, by striking off the call signs of the ships that had been sunk recently. On just two days, the 18th and 19th of October 1940, 28 ships were lost which proved to be the worst two days for shipping losses in the entire war.

The Urla now followed the same path as Jack's previous ship, joining coastal convoys up the East Coast, briefly stopping at Methil, before sailing around northern Britain and arriving at Oban, a major convoy assembly point, on the 2nd of November. For the first time, Jack saw RAF flying boats, which had been based there from the start of the war, taking off and landing. These had recently been upgraded to the more effective Short Sunderland aircraft to carry out maritime patrols, however air cover was extremely limited in range and vast areas of the North Atlantic were unprotected.

Jack and the crew were disappointed to not be allowed any time ashore. In the early hours of the 5th of November, the Urla proceeded into the Atlantic waters, joining the rear of convoy OB.239 which had left Liverpool the previous day, and now comprised 49 merchant vessels, the majority heading for North America and Canada. In the late evening and into the night, Jack and the chief radio officer began to start picking up distress signals from convoy HX.84, which was heading towards them in mid-Atlantic going to Liverpool from Canada, directly west of their route. It turned out that the distress signals were not due to attacks from U-Boats but were because of the German pocket battleship Admiral Scheer, which had entered the North Atlantic unnoticed, with a view to causing as much carnage on merchant vessels as possible. Having sunk a lone cargo ship in the afternoon, the battleship found convoy HX.84 and set about attacking it throughout the evening and night, sinking a total of seven ships. The remaining thirty ships only managed to escape by scattering, following the outstanding bravery of the crew of the Jervis Bay, an old vintage cruise liner escorting the convoy. The Jervis Bay was inadequately armed with seven WW1 guns, and its crew sped directly towards the Admiral Scheer and certain death, to give most of the rest of the convoy valuable time to escape during darkness. This would result in a Victoria Cross for the Captain.

Among the many other acts of bravery during the attack by the Admiral Scheer on HX.84, were those by the crew of the San Demetrio, a British tanker which had loaded 11,200 tons of highly volatile aviation fuel bound for Avonmouth. On that night of the 5th of November, she was hit and set ablaze. The crew escaped on three lifeboats, with the crew in two of them being rescued later. The sixteen men in the third lifeboat found the ship still ablaze two days later but decided to re-board it, gradually bringing the blazes under control, despite the risk of a huge explosion at any moment. Finally getting the engines to run slowly, and without any compass, aids or charts, they risked attack by U-Boats to finally reach the Clyde nine days later having saved 11,000 tons of precious fuel and lost only 200 tons. In 1943, this exceptional act of bravery was made into a successful film, "San Demetrio London" and it became one of the rare films made about the heroism of the Merchant Navy during the war.

By the evening of the 6th of November, as Jack's convoy was now only around ten hours' sailing time from the German battleship's last known area, the Admiralty ordered convoy OB.239 to also disperse. So, the Urla and fifteen other ships headed back to return to Oban, despite the worsening weather of heavy seas and almost gale force winds. Over the next 36 hours the ships laboured their way towards the safety of Scottish waters.

Ploughing through the heavy seas on the early afternoon of the 8th of November, Jack was resting in his cabin when the radio room picked up distress messages that the Swedish freighter Vingaland, from Convoy HX.84, had been fatally bombed around 300 miles astern to the west of them. The planes that had attacked were from a squadron of Condors, long range bombers and maritime reconnaissance planes based in Keil, Germany, which had been sent to find the remainder of Convoy HX.84.

The returning German planes then attacked the Empire Dorado (a British cargo freighter recently bought from American owners) which had struggled to keep up with the Urla and its convoy and was now around 200 miles astern to their west. It received one direct bomb hit. Back in the radio room Jack was now with the chief radio officer David who was on watch. They immediately heard the distress messages from the Empire Dorado stating it was slowly sinking, their lifeboats were smashed and the crew's quarters wrecked. After relaying this to Captain Marsden, he informed them that they were under orders not to stop, and the Empire Dorado was too far away for them to be able to help. The two radio officers felt uneasy about being unable to offer any assistance but were relieved to hear a signal indicating that help was on the way. This was from an unknown ship which turned out to be HMS Lincoln, one of the 50 old WW1 era lend-lease destroyers provided at this time by the Americans, and which were desperately needed by Britain for escort duties. Originally named USS Fairfax, it had only just been transferred to the British Navy that month and was fortunately nearby on its way across the Atlantic with a make-shift crew, to be modified at Plymouth. It picked up the Master and 34 crew and took them safely to Belfast, arriving the following day. Unfortunately, eight of the merchant crew had died immediately from the explosion, and another man died three days later from his wounds. The Empire Dorado was in fact saved from sinking by the armed trawler HMT Man O' War and towed to Rothesay in the Clyde for repairs. Trawlers requisitioned by the Royal Navy during WW2 were given the prefix HMT (His Majesty's Trawler) rather than HMS.

They were still more than 100 miles west of Oban when suddenly, an hour later, the alarm siren went off accompanied by shouts of "enemy aircraft spotted astern". The two gunners rushed to the old Hotchkiss machine gun whilst David, the chief radio officer, started transmitting the aircraft attack signal. Jack - who had rushed out onto deck - saw the rear of the convoy was now being strafed by gunfire. As the rattle of anti-aircraft guns started up from several ships, two German Focke-Wulf Condor planes flying only a few hundred feet above the sea, banked away and started to climb to starboard. When the planes passed by the Urla with their engines roaring, Jack watched their own machine gun hastily firing at the fast-disappearing targets, but both planes swiftly disappeared into the grey clouds unharmed. Going up to the bridge he was astounded to find the Captain standing with an American Tommy machine gun in his hand, cursing not having had a chance to fire it. None of the crew had known he had one on board.

The Urla arrived back in Oban late on that evening the 8th of November, along with the remainder of the convoy unscathed. Jack and the rest of the crew were again confined to the ship, and they soon received orders to recommence their voyage to North America. Correctly believing the German battleship had left the area of their proposed route, the Urla left Oban on the morning of the 10th of November. There was a large British naval task force hunting this German battleship, trying to reduce the huge disruption and congestion it had caused to convoys and Atlantic ports. The Urla joined the rear of another convoy, OB.241, which had departed from Liverpool the previous day. This convoy now comprised 41 ships with six escorts. As these escorts would only be accompanying them for about the next four days - as was the usual pattern - they would be unprotected for several days in the mid-Atlantic. It wasn't however the German forces which would be their next obstacle.

By the time the convoy had reached the dangerous mid-ocean area the weather had started to become increasingly wild, with waves of 40-60 feet high, lashing rain, and strong winds. The further west the convoy sailed the stronger the storm grew, and gradually the ships became separated as their speeds varied or dropped. Conditions on board the Urla made even a simple task almost impossible as the ship rose and fell at an alarming rate. There were several falls and injuries as various articles became loose and flew around, and going on deck was restricted to only urgent tasks. Incredibly no one was swept overboard. For several days sleeping and eating became increasing difficult, even for the most experienced seamen. Sitting on his bolted-down chair while bent over his table, Jack found even writing in the wireless log virtually impossible.

Suddenly, on the evening of the 26th of November, Jack picked up two distress signals from the forty-year-old Greek freighter Eugena Cambanis, asking other ships in the area to indicate their position. It went on to say that their steering mechanism was wrecked, their engines had stopped, and the holds were filling with water. Four days previously, this ship loaded with timber had left Nova Scotia in Canada, in a slow convoy (SC.13) heading for Liverpool. But due to the storm the ship had only managed 150 miles and was now struggling in what had become hurricane winds, with wild sea conditions. In fact, all this convoy was seriously hit by the storm and became scattered, with five ships returning to Nova Scotia within a few days. Another ship, the Kolchis, had sent out a distress call not long after leaving port, then nothing further was heard as she disappeared beneath the waves with all hands. A further distress call was picked up by Jack around the same time on the evening of the 26th from the freighter Lisieux, stating that they were floundering and taking on water, with their cargo of wood pulp expanding, causing the metal plates in the hull to crack.

Jack urgently reported the distress calls to Captain Marsden. After checking their positions on the charts, he gave Jack the order to break radio silence. Jack was to transmit a message to the Greek ship Eugena Cambanis, saying that they were standing by, and although they were only twenty miles away, due to the weather conditions they were limited to two knots. The risk that U-Boats could pick up this message was considered worth taking. Another ship, the Norwegian Bernhard, indicated it would attempt to rescue the crew of the Lisieux which was further north, around the same time.

Maintaining radio contact, by the following morning the Urla had managed to creep close to the stricken Greek freighter, so that the highly difficult transfer of the crew could begin, while ensuring that their own ship was just far enough away to avoid a collision. A lifeboat was launched from the freighter with the 28 crew aboard. They somehow managed to safely steer themselves to the side of the Urla, while bobbing around like a cork in the huge waves. Tying a rope from the Urla around their waists as a safety measure, over the next hour all the Greek crew finally managed to grab hold of the rope ladder which dangled down from the side of the Urla. Thankfully, they then succeeded in climbing aboard without getting swept away. Last of all, the Greek Captain Economidis came aboard in great pain due to a back injury, and the Urla could finally steam away from the danger of the partly sunk stricken freighter. It would remain afloat due to its timber cargo, until shelled and sunk by a Norwegian freighter the following month, as it was a danger to shipping.

Still battling the storm, and now amid sleet and snow falls, on Monday the 2nd of December the Urla finally reached St. John's in Newfoundland, Canada, which was the nearest North American port to Britain over 2,000 miles away. Undermining the strategic importance of Newfoundland, and close to St. John's, was the Bay Roberts Relay Station. This was where undersea telegraph cables from England linked the U.S.A. to Britain, including a private line from Prime Minister Churchill to President Roosevelt.

The survivors from the Lisieux had landed at St. John's during the weekend before Jack's arrival. They were rescued and brought to Canada on board the Norwegian ship Bernhard. Many of the crew of the Lisieux had not been so fortunate. One lifeboat had been picked up containing seventeen survivors, but tragically two more had died in that lifeboat which had drifted for hours in the storm. Another sailor had somehow survived alone for 24 hours in the other remaining lifeboat which was swept away when the rest of the crew were trying to get onboard, before he was then picked up on the verge of collapse. Tragically ten of the crew were unable to get off the ship and then drowned. The survivors who landed in St. John's were just some of over 6,000 seamen who would be landed there safely during WW2.

Having taken on provisions and coal, the Urla was able to leave St. John's on the 8th of December, once the snow had ceased and the freezing temperatures eased, allowing the build-up of ice to be removed from the ship's deck and superstructure. From here they steamed about 350 miles southwest to the port of Sydney, in Nova Scotia, which was second only to Halifax, Nova Scotia, as a convoy assembly point for the UK. It was at Sydney that the Urla would pick up her valuable cargo of steel for the return journey, plus some timber pit props.

Sydney, with its well sheltered harbour, had one of the world's largest steel plants, producing 43 percent of Canada's steel. This steel plant was fed by coal from numerous nearby coal mines, plus the largest high-grade iron ore mines in the British Empire, which were located at Bell Island, Newfoundland. It was from here that the eastbound slower convoys to the U.K. would commence. These were the SC convoys, comprising ships travelling at a maximum of 8 knots. However, the crew of the Urla were delighted to receive the news that one week after their cargo had finished being loaded, they would be heading southwest approximately 600 miles, to Boston in the USA for some repairs to the engines. On the 21st of December they arrived at Boston where the temperature was several degrees warmer than at St John's, and life was carrying as normal, with America still neutral. The crew looked forward to some time away from the war, for some entertainment and with no blackouts.

One of the most well-known drinking and entertainment establishments in the city was The Silver Dollar Bar on Washington Street, near the dock area. It proclaimed it had the world's longest bar, and with its modestly priced dining, a dance floor and a bandstand, it was hugely popular. As the war progressed, dock workers, naval personnel and seamen from around the world flocked to the bar. The pre-war vaudeville acts were replaced with non-stop jazz bands and singers, playing at an increasingly loud volume. The atmosphere became volatile at times, with heavy drinking and fights, but Jack and most of the crew survived their visits there.

However, one night a couple of the stokers were returned to their ship in a dishevelled drunken state courtesy of the American Navy shore patrol and promptly fined by the Captain.

Jack and a couple of the officers were invited to the home of a retired American naval officer and his family, for Christmas. On visiting his home in the suburbs, they were amazed by the expanse of food and drink on offer, and by the size and variety of modern appliances in this house. Their final few days in the city were spent shopping for some gifts to take back home, seeing a movie or appreciating one of the many big band acts in the theatre district.

Their brief spell of relaxation soon ended, as on New Year's Eve the Urla departed Boston, to steam back northwards to the main convoy assembly port of Halifax, Canada. Eventually, after a wait of nine days and with her stocks of coal replenished, the Urla left Halifax on the 11th of January 1941, sailing at the rear of Convoy HX.102, which comprised 26 cargo ships, with almost half of them loaded with steel like the Urla. From the moment the convoy set sail it was subject to heavy winds and snow, which over the first week would increase to gale force. Within the first couple of days two ships would be forced to return to Halifax with steering problems and leaks. On board the Urla things were not going well from the start. Fully laden with 6,800 tons of steel and lumber, coupled with the poor-quality coal which they had just loaded at Halifax, the ship struggled to keep up speed, and they were unable to make more than four and a half knots. By nighttime on the first day, they had lost the rest of the convoy. The coal they used the following day seemed to be of a better quality, allowing them to increase their speed to nine knots. Despite this increase in pace and having the instructions for the convoy's route, they were unable to find the rest of the convoy, despite knowing what its predicted position should be for the first three days. Yet again, on the 14th of January they found they were using inferior coal, so their speed dropped to four knots. At dinner, the Captain informed the officers that with a strong westerly gale now blowing it would be almost impossible to turn back, so there was no choice but to proceed independently. Furthermore, the Captain explained that if he followed their routing instructions it would be impossible to reach their destination of Manchester, on account of the dreadful coal and the consumption of it needing to be so heavy. He therefore proposed to set a direct course to pass the north of Ireland rather than the more southerly Atlantic route which the rest of their convoy would use. Several ships would subsequently be joining them from another convoy travelling from Bermuda.

There followed an increasingly anxious time over the next two weeks, as they struggled alone through the storm. They knew they were approaching the area which was under the greatest threat from the U-Boats to the north and west of Ireland, whilst also becoming increasingly concerned about the dwindling coal stocks. By the 28th of January, as the gale had subsided, the crew began to mix wood with their remaining coal supplies, hoping to get better results. However, they were still almost 400 miles from the coast of Ireland and managing only four and a half knots.

Suddenly at 19.40 hours, in the pervasive blackness beneath the cloudy sky, there was a loud explosion and a bright flash, followed almost immediately by a huge wave of seawater rising up and over the port side of the ship, 70 feet from the bow. As the ship shuddered violently, Jack, who was talking with a colleague outside his cabin, knew immediately that they had been torpedoed. He grabbed his coat and lifejacket, and ran to the radio room, as the siren started to blast its warning to the crew. Arriving at the radio room, the chief officer Peter asked Jack to check their exact position with the Captain, using the voice pipe. Their position of latitude

54 degrees north and longitude 19.20 degrees west, was close to where Jack was sunk just a few months ago. A distress message was ordered to be sent out several times, as the Captain continued to receive reports of the damage.

The hatch covers and beams had been blown away from number two hold, along with the front part of the bridge and the steel wheelhouse. It was clear that although the Urla had remained on an even keel, she was rapidly filling with water and going down by the head with her heavy steel cargo. The Captain quickly gave the order to abandon ship and muster at the two undamaged aft lifeboats. Jack's last duty was to collect the confidential log and code books, put them all in a weighted bag and throw it overboard on his way aft. Miraculously, everyone was accounted for. They all safely transferred into the boats and proceeded to pull away from the ship in the moderate swell and wind, to avoid any dangerous eddies when the ship sank. No sooner had they reached a safe distance when the Urla's bows went down. The stern raised up to almost vertical, and she disappeared under a huge bubble and swirl of water. With the last of the steam blowing off, and loose wreckage shooting to the surface, the ship had gone down within twenty minutes of being hit, leaving an eerie silence as the crew sat and pondered their fate.

Jack sat tightly in the Captain's boat with 27 others, whilst the smaller lifeboat held the other 14 crew, with the First Mate in charge. It was agreed that they would all remain in the area for the time being, with the two boats connected by a rope, as they knew their distress call had been acknowledged by a shore-based radio station. After a long and cramped night with little sleep, dawn finally broke just after 9am. Bringing the two boats together, the Captain and the First Mate checked on everyone's condition and what supplies each boat had. They estimated that it would take approximately four to five days to reach the Irish coast, if conditions remained reasonably moderate with a following wind. The lifeboats' provisions were organised accordingly, so that each day, every person was allocated six hard tack biscuits, some malted milk tablets, around half a small tin of pemmican, (a chewy dried mixture of pounded beef and fat with a few currants), two small squares of chocolate and four measured cups of water.

Orders were given for the men to change positions every two hours, to help to avoid cramp and give a bit more space to the men who were injured. After the members of the crew were assigned to navigation, steering, lookouts, stores or bailing duties, at 10.00 hours on the 29th of January the two boats set sail to the east. Not long after setting off there was a call from one of the lookouts. The crew soon realised that what they could see was two submarines on the surface moving to the northeast, about two miles away. Although their lifeboats must also have been spotted by the submarines' crews, the submarines did not stop or approach them and were soon lost to view.

Still making reasonable progress, at about 15.00 hours one of the crew spotted smoke from a ship sailing across their intended path. The Captain ordered one of the red distress flares to be lit and the crew cheered as the ship turned towards them. As it got closer it turned out to be a large passenger liner which had been altered to become an armed merchant cruiser with several guns fitted to it. Everyone in the lifeboats assumed it had picked up their S.O.S. and was looking for them. When it drew close to them it slowed and signalled to them, asking which ship they were from. Following the reply, the cruiser's crew replied that help was coming, then they picked up speed and disappeared over the horizon. All the men in the two lifeboats were hugely disappointed, and several of them were cursing. The reason for the ship's swift departure became more obvious an hour later. As the light began to fade, another submarine was sighted in the distance, heading towards them, but then thankfully it turned away to the west and disappeared.

As darkness fell, the wind started to blow hard, rain squalls arrived and the mood in the lifeboats worsened. Jack was at least glad he had taken his heavy overcoat with him, as this gave him some protection from the miserable weather, a valuable lesson he had learned from his previous sinking. In view of the deteriorating weather conditions the Captain ordered the boats to hove to and deploy their sea anchors. These were not traditional anchors, but were wide canvas cones, about two feet in diameter and several feet long to act as a drag. These anchors were attached by a line to the lifeboat to keep the boats head or stern to the wind and sea, preventing them from getting broadside on. Also attached to the trailing line nearer the stern of their boats was a perforated canvas bag containing a wad of oakum (rope fibres soaked in vegetable or fish oil) which gave off a thin oil slick, thereby reducing the wave force and the amount of water splashing into the boats.

The night was long, cold, wet, tiring, cramped and extremely uncomfortable, particularly for those with injuries. Several of the crew were seasick from the continuous buffeting of the waves, and proper sleep was impossible. During the night the two lifeboats became separated. Fortunately, at 7am the next day (the 31st of January) Jack's lifeboat was spotted by the large convoy SL.62, despite being in darkness. This convoy consisted of thirty ships heading to Britain from Freetown, West Africa, and just the day before had been attacked by German bombers. Two of the convoy's ships had been sunk, and there were numerous reports of enemy submarines in the area, so stopping to rescue anyone else was fraught with danger. Luckily for Jack and the crew in his boat, the steam freighter SS Siris (a Royal Mail Line ship carrying cereals and cottonseed) did stop for them, and they hurriedly boarded. The lifeboat had managed to sail roughly half of the distance towards Ireland, but the crew were delighted to finally leave it behind. Before he got himself comfortable in the mess, Captain Marsden immediately informed the master of the Siris that their other lifeboat was also somewhere in that area, and a message was sent to one of the escorts to search for it. The rescued crew felt immense relief as they dried out, had some hot food and drinks, and soon fell asleep. Fortunately, with the British Naval escorts that had just arrived from Britain to accompany them, they all covered the remainder of the journey without incident.

On the morning of the 2nd of February 1941 Jack stepped ashore at Oban, Scotland, almost three months after he had left there. He felt very relieved, but also disappointed that he had not yet completed a successful round trip. He wondered, no doubt like many other Merchant sailors, if they were being overwhelmed by the enemy. As if to reinforce the point, the fourteen crew on board the other lifeboat, which had separated from them during the night, saw another submarine on the surface that following morning. Thankfully, they had also been picked up and subsequently landed at Londonderry, Northern Ireland on the 5th of February. They had been rescued by one of the convoy's escorts, HMT Northern Dawn. This was one of hundreds of fishing trawlers that had been converted into armed rescue and escort vessels which were operating within three days' sailing of British ports.

The original convoy HX.102, which Jack had been with from Halifax on the 11th of January, safely reached Liverpool without any attacks on the 29th of January. This was the day after Jack was torpedoed. Had it not been for the combination of the storms and the bad coal reducing their speed, leading to them becoming separated from the rest of the convoy and therefore an easy target, they too could have had a successful voyage. However, what Jack never knew throughout his life was that the submarine that did sink them was not German but Italian and named Luigi Torelli.

The Italian Navy, the Regia Marina, had entered the war on the 10th of June 1940, just before the fall of France. They had one of the world's largest submarine fleets, among them 62 ocean going vessels. In the autumn of 1940, a flotilla of Italian submarines began to be deployed from the Mediterranean to Betasom. Betasom was the code word for their newly acquired base at Bordeaux in the southwest of France, situated about sixty miles up the River Garonne from the Atlantic coast. By the end of 1940, the Italian Navy had relocated 27 submarines there. Although many of these submarines had been built recently, in many ways they were unsuitable for operations in the North Atlantic, having been designed primarily for surface cruising and engagement in the calmer, warmer Mediterranean waters. They were generally larger with bigger superstructures than U-Boats making moveability poorer. In addition, they had lower speeds, whether diving, underwater or cruising, and there were issues with lack of up-to-date equipment. However, many of these shortcomings were quickly overcome, and these Italian submarines proved to be effective additional reinforcements for the Germans, sinking around one million tons of Allied shipping.

The submarine Luigi Torelli that attacked Jack's ship arrived at the Bordeaux base on the 5th of October 1940, having completed trials. It was one of the latest Italian submarines, having only been commissioned in May 1940. On the 9th of November Primo Longobardo took command of this submarine. Longobardo had recently gained exceptional experience in the North Atlantic, having returned from a patrol on board U-99, which was commanded by Otto Kretschmer, the most successful U-Boat German commander of the whole war. In November, Primo Longobardo's first patrol off the northwest coast of Ireland was unsuccessful, due to severe weather and problems with the primary electric motors. However, this would change on his next patrol, as Jack would discover.

On the 9th of January 1941 the Luigi Torelli had sailed from Bordeaux to patrol the sea west of Scotland, two days before the Urla left Halifax, Canada. On the evening of the 15th of January, the submarine successfully torpedoed two Greek ships and a Norwegian vessel on the outward-bound convoy OB.272. Five days later the submarine tried to attack two British destroyers during separate attacks but was unsuccessful in both. On the 22nd of January, Primo Longobardo was ordered to move about 70 miles south, and it was here on the morning of the 28th of January 1941 that they spotted the smoke from the Urla in the far distance. Tracking the ship for nine hours and finally closing in to within 400 metres they fired a single torpedo which sunk Jack's ship. This was the final engagement of the patrol by the Italian submarine, which eventually returned to Bordeaux on the 6th of February. This was one day after Jack had reported to the Marconi office in Hull, having travelled back to his home city after his safe arrival in Oban. Jack was granted special leave again, of two weeks, plus annual leave until the 5th of March.

MESSAGE T.O.R. 1455/8 November.
Date 8.11.40.
Recd. 1525

From   Scapa W/T.

P/L BY T/P

Addressed Admiralty.
IMPORTANT
Following received on 500 KC/s.
55 7 N 16 50 W.
G L Z K EMPIRE DORADO sinking slowly no means of getting away
all lifeboats smashed two rafts still alongside help urgently
required casualties aboard GLZK.

T.O.R. 1455/8
Advance Copy Ops., O.D.Trade.

1st Lord.
1st S.L.   Ops. (4).
V.C.N.S.   O.D.(3).
A.C.N.S.(H).   D.T.D.(2).
A.C.N.S.(T).   D.T.D. Basement.
NAV. SEC.   Cdr. Holbrook.   R.G. of S.S.
PARL. SEC.   D.T.M.   Salvage.
C.S.O. to 1st S.L.   D. of S.T.   W.D.
D.A/S.W.   O.I.C.(2).   Press Division.
M.(2).   D.S.D.9.   C.C.R.T.
D.N.I.(4).   I.P.(3).

'Radio message regarding sinking of Empire Dorado, after being attacked in Jack's convoy OB.239, 8th November 1940' (Kew National Archives)

2359/8th November.
FROM: H.M.S.LINCOLN.   Date: 9.11.40.
                                    Recd: 0445.
        Naval Cypher C by W/T.

ADDRESSED: C. in C. Western Approaches, Admiralty,
           C. in C. Home Fleet.

    Regret owing to bad weather and ?poor visibility
unable to locate any survivors of H X 84 H.M.S.LINCOLN
has however on board master and 34 survivors of S.S.
EMPIRE DORA.

                    2359/8.

                    Advance Copy Ops. O.D. O.I.C.
                                         Trade.
1st Lord.
1st S.L.   D.S.D.9.
V.C.N.S.   D.N.I.(4)   D.P.D.
A.C.N.S.(H)   M.(2)   I.P.(3)
A.C.N.S.(L)   D.T.D.(2)   File X.
A.C.N.S.(T)   D.T.D.Basement.
Naval Sec.   D. of P.(3)
Parl.Sec.   Admiral Bailey.
C.S.O. to 1st S.L.   D.A/S.W.
Ops.(4)   Cdr.Holbrook.

'Radio message from H.M.S. Lincoln after rescuing crew from Empire Dorado, 9th November 1940' (Kew National Archives)

'SS Urla' (Marsh Maritime Museum)

'Christmas period 1940, Siver Dollar Bar,
Boston.

Jack on the right' (Author's)

'Steel works at Sydney, Nova Scotia, Canada, where cargo was loaded, December 1940'
(Nova Scotia Archives, colour Grant Kemp).

'Convoy formation, Bedford Basin, Halifax, Nova Scotia, Canada'
(Nova Scotia Archives, colour Grant Kemp).

'Italian submarine Luigi Torelli arriving back at its base at Betasom, Bordeaux,
France, having sunk the Urla one week previously, early February 1941'
(regiamarina.net, colour by Grant Kemp)

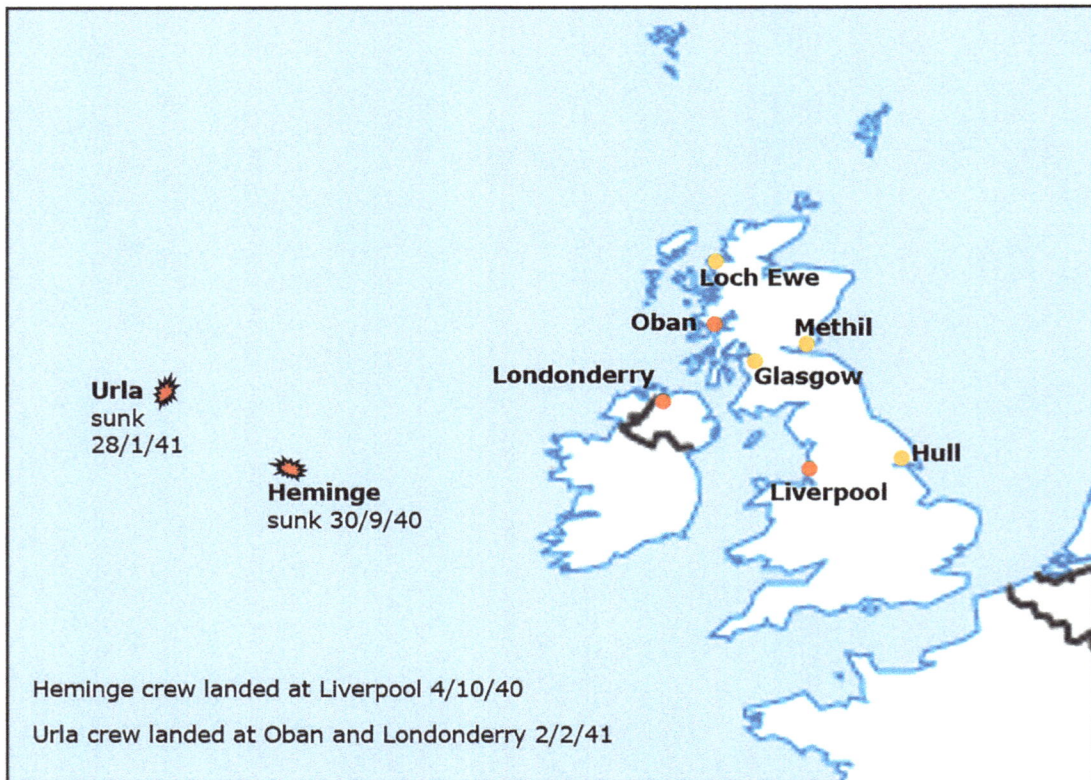

'Map showing positions of sinkings of the Heminge and Urla'
(Author's)

Chapter 5
SS Kingswood

In early 1941 every aspect of life was visibly changing for the population of Britain. People had to make large adjustments with regards to food, as there was a decreasing amount of food available due to rationing. During his leave in February, Jack had heard from his brother-in-law (a fish merchant in the city) that the effects on the fishing industry were huge, particularly in Hull. Most of the commercial fishing boats had been requisitioned by the Admiralty. The larger and faster trawler boats were fitted out for anti-submarine duties, convoy escorts and rescue work. Older boats were used for minesweeping, harbour boom defences and depot ship duties. Casualties were high for the remaining fishing vessels which were also targeted by the Germans. The North Sea fishing grounds were severely restricted, and fishermen moved further westwards off the coasts of Ireland, Scotland and Iceland. Hull's trawler fleet of 191 vessels in 1939 was reduced by half by the end of the war, with even greater reductions in Grimsby and other east coast ports. Although fish was never rationed, catches in 1941 were down to one third of pre-war levels. This led to prices rising to four to five times the amount for the popular catches such as haddock, cod and plaice, until price controls were introduced later that year. In addition to Jack's father's income from his work at the Co-Op, Jack contributed financially to the household. Likewise, his sister Gwen who worked in an insurance office brought her wages into the family, as although she was married, she was still living at home with Jack and their parents. This meant that they were in a better financial position than some friends and neighbours, who had lost family members and their homes.

While Jack was home during February, there were eight light bombing attacks on Hull, killing a total of 21 people and seriously injuring 39 others. There were alerts almost daily but compared to other cities they had so far been fortunate. Despite having had a disastrous start to his role as a radio officer, with his first two ships being sunk without completing their voyages, he waited restlessly at night by the family's back door. Looking up at the sky, he told his sister that he would rather be at sea than here at home, enduring the warning sirens, waiting for yet another air raid. Regardless, the risk of air raids did not stop people from making the most of enjoying themselves. Jack, like many others on leave, went to some of the numerous popular dances put on throughout the war, which were often used to raise money for those in distress. During this period of leave, Jack together with family and friends, attended one dance held at the grand Edwardian Beverley Road swimming baths. The pool was boarded over to make a temporary dance floor for the five hundred or so people who attended, and this dance was run by the Co-Op where his father worked. These dances were so popular that they were held three times a week, and this place was just one of many such entertainment locations in the city.

Jack again replaced his lost luggage, clothing and personal effects in nervous anticipation of his next voyage. During his leave he caught up with the remainder of his family and friends.

Although his closest old school friend Sam Burwell was not on leave, Jack was delighted to hear from his parents that Sam had just been awarded the Distinguished Service Medal for his actions in Norway ten months ago. However Sam was now serving in the Mediterranean, and it would be the following year before they met again. Reporting at the Marconi office he was pleased to hear that his next ship would be leaving from Hull, and it would be the SS Kingswood. Jack was informed that this was a cargo ship of a similar size to the Urla, around 5,000 tons with a speed of 10.5 knots. The Kingswood had been launched in 1929 and was owned by the Constantine Steamship Company, who had a good reputation with seamen for their overall conditions.

Jack discovered that the crew of 48 was mainly British and very amiable. There were several men from Hull and Yorkshire, including the first radio officer, 22-year-old Peter Mitchell. Many others were from the North East of England including the 41-year-old Captain, Fredrick Fenn. Finally, Jack would have a trouble-free period at sea despite the mounting shipping losses. It later transpired that he was fortunate to have left Hull when he did, in early March 1941, as he would discover on his return just over two months later.

The Kingswood left Hull docks independently on the 11th of March in ballast, to steam the short distance north to the River Tyne. During this time, ships were provided with safety measures against the deadly magnetic mines laid in the thousands by the Germans, especially in the estuaries and along the east coast of Britain since the start of the war. This was known as degaussing, whereby larger ships were fitted with a thick copper cable around the whole of the inside of the ship. Having measured the magnetic field of the ship, a large electrical current was transferred into it, to neutralise and overcome detection by these mines. However, an alternative method was used for the Kingswood, which was known as wiping. For this procedure, the ship was brought alongside a shore degaussing station where a cable was lowered to the keel. Then the current was switched on to neutralise the ship's plates. This was a far quicker method as several ships could be completed in a day. This saved vast amounts of valuable copper but had to be repeated every six months to be effective. There were still unavoidable threats from the many contact mines also laid by the Germans, as the crew of the Kingswood soon discovered on leaving the Humber Estuary when a mine was seen floating past them. The Captain gave the gun crew permission to open fire on the mine with their machine guns. After several hundred rounds were fired, and by now almost out of sight, it finally exploded to ironic cheers from the rest of the crew.

Although this short, first part of the voyage lasted only twelve hours it was in an area of constant danger to shipping. In addition to the danger of mines, the Luftwaffe were carrying out regular sorties and some U-Boats were still operating close by. During this week that the Kingswood was waiting on the Tyne for the rest of the convoy to arrive, two ships and one tug had been mined and sunk, one cargo ship was bombed, and another sunk by a U-Boat. All these attacks were along this one-hundred-mile stretch of coastal water from the Humber to the Tyne.

Finally, on the 18th of March, they all left in a coastal convoy to steam around Scotland. Although no attacks occurred and the weather was generally calm, albeit unusually cold for the time of year, for two nights fog descended. This presented yet another danger, as there were 32 ships sailing in close formation. Fortunately, all reached Oban safely ready for the ensuing Atlantic crossing. The following day the Kingswood steamed out from the harbour to join convoy OB.301, and the crew were delighted to learn that their destination was to be New York. Although Jack heard several distress calls from Allied ships these were from locations further north towards Iceland. The convoy dispersed after four days, and the Kingswood reached American waters safely on the 9th of April.

As the Kingswood approached the Hudson River, an American pilot came aboard and had the customary drink with the Captain. He guided the Kingswood to a berth near one of the huge grain elevators, where it was to load its vital return cargo, as the UK was at that time taking almost half of all American wheat exports. By coincidence, on that same day Jack and some of the crew were able to tune in and listen to the BBC broadcast from London of Winston Churchill making a speech in the House of Commons, reviewing the war. Churchill concluded:

"Once we have gained the Battle of the Atlantic and are sure of the constant flow of American supplies which are being prepared for us, then, however far Hitler may go or whatever new millions and scores of millions he may lap in misery, we who are armed with the sword of retributive justice shall be on his track."

Although America was still neutral, the American opinion was gradually turning in favour of increasing support for Britain. Conversely, there was a vocal minority who opposed this. All the news outlets made this very clear to the ship's crew during their time in New York. On the 21st of April, the famous aviator Charles Lindbergh, who had made the first solo non-stop flight across the Atlantic in 1927, addressed a large crowd in the city. He was a member of the isolationist pressure group, America First Committee, who were against America becoming involved in foreign wars.

Jack encountered only good wishes during their forced extended stay in the city, which was caused by a problem with the telemotor. The telemotor was a hydraulic device linking the ship's wheel to the rear steering gear, and its failure had resulted in the ship hitting a sandy shoal on the river. This in turn required a full assessment by Lloyd's ship inspectors to confirm it was still seaworthy. As a result of this delay the Kingswood spent 18 days in port which coincided with a period of several days of warm temperatures between 75-85 degrees Fahrenheit. So all the crew took full advantage of the warmth and the time they now had to explore the city. This gave them a welcome break from the war - once they had been registered and fingerprinted.

With an exchange rate of four dollars to the pound, and away from the strict rationing in Britain, Jack and some of the officers headed into the city. First, they sent telegrams to their families stating that they had arrived safely, then they took advantage of the wide variety of food, drink and late-night entertainment available at affordable prices. Shopping visits to acquire items rationed or no longer available in Britain were popular, and everyone bought sweets and chocolates to take back home. In addition, Jack purchased small bottles of perfume for his sisters, realising that these could easily stay in his coat pockets if he had to abandon ship again. One afternoon they decided to visit the Yankee Stadium to see a baseball game for their first time, with the New York Yankees playing Philadelphia Athletics. Unknown to the British officers, among the Yankee players was Joe DiMaggio. The following month DiMaggio began the record for the longest hitting streak in major league baseball across 56 consecutive games, from May the 15th to July the 16th 1941. He became regarded as the greatest player of all time and subsequently married Marilyn Munroe.

Not surprisingly, some of the crew overindulged and returned on board worse for wear, or reported late and were fined a day's wages, and one of the firemen absconded. Another man fell overboard into the Hudson River whilst the ship was moving down stream to load their cargo, but fortunately he was picked up by a tug. Before the grain cargo could be loaded, and to prevent it from shifting, wooden bulkheads were erected in each hold, running fore and aft. Then once loading was completed and a replacement fireman had signed on, the Kingswood departed New York on the 27ᵗʰ of April. Two days later, at the convoy port of Halifax, Canada, Jack reflected that it had been only just over three months since he had previously left this port before being torpedoed. Jack was yet to successfully complete a return trip and was secretly praying that he would finally have some good luck.

The next day, once the Kingswood had taken on addition coal supplies, the ship left port, in convoy HX.124 along with 37 merchant vessels, eleven of which contained fuel and oils which were always a high value target for the U-Boats. For Jack it was back to tiring watches but at least the weather was forecast to be reasonably calm for the crossing, and the routine on board ship quickly took over. During the first week, several messages were picked up from ships that had been attacked by U-Boats, but these were all towards the western approaches of Britain, and the convoy proceeded without any incidents. It was still possible for the radio room to pick up American radio stations which provided a welcome distraction with their news and dance music. In between watches there were plenty of magazines and books amongst the crew that had come from their time in New York, which they could swap and share. Card games such as pontoon and crib were always popular. The men made regular visits to the engine room to fire steam into a bucket for instant hot water, for washing clothes or bathing.

Steadily heading northeast after ten days of sailing, Jack's convoy caught up with and joined convoy SC.30, a slower moving convoy of 28 merchant ships, 20 miles ahead, heading for Liverpool. Both convoys were now south of Greenland and approaching another dangerous area where U-Boats were operating. The convoy commander received instructions from the Western Approaches command centre (recently relocated from Plymouth to a secure basement in Derby House Liverpool), to significantly alter course by 100 degrees to port, taking them further north towards Iceland. Unfortunately, a thick fog descended, lasting for 17 hours, and after considerable confusion most ships finally managed to return to their stations within their respective convoys.

Unfortunately, on the morning of 13th May, one escort ship from SC.30, HMS Salopian, a passenger liner of 10,500 tons, which was now being utilised as an armed merchant cruiser, was spotted by U-98, but despite it firing four torpedoes, they all missed. The submarine gave chase on the surface and an hour later, despite the fog, it spotted the Salopian. The U-Boat then fired two more torpedoes which hit their target, despite the Salopian returning fire. The ship remained afloat whilst all but three of the crew safely disembarked into ten lifeboats. Eventually, after firing a final torpedo as a coup de grace, the ship was sunk, four and a half hours after the attack had begun. Luckily for the survivors, the destroyer HMS Impulsive picked up the 278 surviving crew members. The previous year, the Impulsive had made four return trips to Dunkirk and rescued almost 3,000 men, and now it was part of the growing mid-Atlantic escort group based in Iceland.

On board the Kingswood, in convoy HX.124, around 400 miles south-east of Cape Farewell, the southernmost point of Greenland, Jack picked up the distress calls from the Salopian. He informed the Captain about this, as they were only 30 miles astern. All gun crews remained on alert during the afternoon. Fortunately, the only other distress calls were from some distance away, to the west of Ireland, but tensions remained high on board the Kingswood. Four days later, in the morning when Jack was still asleep, the alarm for action stations went off. They were 200 miles south of Iceland when all the escorting ships' guns opened fire at a Focke Wolfe Condor plane approaching the convoy, which then turned away and disappeared. (Later that day the radio room picked up distress signals from the cargo ship Statesman which had been bombed and sunk by a Condor plane around 300 miles southeast of them). The commander of the convoy gave the order to alter course southwards until dark, by four long blasts on the siren, in case of further enemy aircraft. Deciding he would not get back to sleep before his next watch started, Jack went up to the bridge to talk to and help the lookouts. After an hour with no further sightings, he was about to leave to carry out some chores when the ship rocked and shook violently. Several pairs of depth charges had been released by one of the escorts, and even though they were around half a mile away, the tremors could be felt. The force of the underwater blasts on board the Kingswood came as a surprise to Jack, so he held onto a rail because he was expecting further jolts, as some of the other escorts started criss-crossing an area of the sea to their rear. Thankfully, no more jolts were forthcoming and indeed there are no records of any submarines sunk on that day.

It was a great relief to the crew when they approached the Scottish coast and were ordered to enter Loch Ewe on the 19th of May. It was a calm, dry, bright day for Jack's first visit to this large convoy staging area in the Northwest Highlands. During their 19-day voyage across the North Atlantic, ten cargo ships from other convoys had been lost on a similar northerly arched route past Greenland and Iceland. A further thirteen were sunk to the south of them, mainly sailing independently, in the Western Approaches. In peacetime, the normal direct route from Halifax, Canada would have taken about a week and would have been 700 miles shorter.

Loch Ewe is a sheltered sea loch, two and a half miles at its widest and seven miles long. It lies between two peninsulas which provide a mile-wide entrance and has good depth for the safe anchorage of almost 100 vessels. With just a handful of small villages nearby, and crofting and fishing communities around its shores, it was a sparsely populated area. The nearest large town was Inverness, 80 miles away to the southeast and the nearest train station was at Achnasheen, 40 miles inland, connected by a single-track road with passing places. Its isolation therefore made it the perfect location to be used as an anchorage, and it was further away for the German planes to have to travel to attack them. Loch Ewe was used by the Royal Navy for the first few months of the war, as it was felt that the main Navy base at Scapa Flow did not yet have adequate defences, following the sinking of the battleship Royal Oak there. The home fleet was therefore spread between the Clyde, Loch Ewe and the River Forth at Rosyth. Although on the 4th of December 1939 the battleship HMS Nelson was damaged by a magnetic mine entering Loch Ewe, no enemy submarines managed to get inside the loch during the war.

The use of Loch Ewe by the Merchant Navy had gradually increased over the 18 months prior to Jack's arrival on board the Kingswood. Many of these Merchant ships had come from the crowded port of Oban, which now had about one third fewer convoy vessels. Full anti-submarine boom nets and guard loops with controlled mines had been put in place near the entrance of Loch Ewe, together with some naval and anti-aircraft guns defences onshore. At that time only the Merchant ships' captains were allowed onshore, for convoy conferences, and the rest of the crew were not permitted to go ashore to send telegrams or letters by post. There were restrictions on loading provisions, stores, fuel and water, unless urgently required, due to heavy demand at all ports. Armed yachts led merchant ships to their anchorages which were to the southward side of the loch, with a hospital ship and depot ships anchored near the shore.

Naval convoy escort ships were anchored to the east of the small Isle of Ewe within the loch. The defences continued to be gradually improved as the loch grew in importance, with up to 3,000 personnel involved there. From early 1942 some of the Arctic convoys to Russia also began to gather there.

The day after their arrival, the 20ᵗʰ of May, the Kingswood left to join convoy WN.129 heading for the east coast of Britain, which had left the Clyde the day before. After stopping in Methil on the River Forth where they waited offshore, they finally arrived back in Hull on the 24ᵗʰ of May. Jack was thrilled that finally he had completed a return trip safely.

Jack had been extremely fortunate in the timings of his voyages, to have avoided three major calamities that happened during his ten weeks away from March to May 1941. The German Navy planned and carried out several raids by its modern surface battle fleet against Allied shipping in the North Atlantic, at the end of 1940 and early 1941. These raids supplemented their submarine attacks in the exact areas Jack was transversing between North America and Britain. Operation Berlin involved the battleships Scharnhorst and Gneisenau, which successfully attacked or captured 22 Allied merchant vessels, during January to March 1941. Ten of these merchant ships were sunk about 500 miles east of Newfoundland, on the 16ᵗʰ of March. Two weeks later Jack passed through this same area heading towards New York, having avoided being involved in these disasters, by the providential timing of his crossing.

Secondly in May 1941, during operation Rheinubung, the Bismarck and Prinz Eugen proceeded to break into the North Atlantic from Norway through the Denmark Straits between Iceland and Greenland. On the same day that Jack returned to Hull, the British battleship HMS Hood was sunk in that area. The continuing naval engagement over the next few days resulted in the sinking of the Bismarck. The Bismarck was sunk in the area that Jack's convoy had been in, just two weeks beforehand. So ended German battleship operations in the Atlantic, and yet again Jack was lucky to have avoided being in the vicinity of the battle.

The final event that Jack was fortunate to miss during his time away at sea, happened during the sudden increase in huge bomber raids on many of the seaports of Britain, especially during the first week of May 1941, when Liverpool, Belfast, Greenock and Hull were targeted. The destruction in Hull was immediately apparent to the crew of the Kingswood, as they approached the docks along the River Humber. More than 2,500 feet of the riverside quay at the Albert Docks was severely damaged, and adjacent fruit sheds were destroyed, together with most of the cargo sheds along the adjacent William Wright Docks. Most of the docks in Hull received some damage, more so on the western side, including numerous buildings and offices, dock walls, jetties, warehouses, sheds, railway sidings, coal hoists and timber stacks. Several barges, small boats and a minesweeper had been sunk, which added to the chaos. Luckily for the Kingswood and the Vera Radcliffe, which were two of the five ships steaming into Hull together, two of the city's large flour mills were still operating. This meant that although five flour mills had been destroyed, including the imposing Rank Mill on the junction of the River Hull and Victoria Docks, the two ships were still able to offload their cargoes of grain.

Whilst Jack had been away, Hull had been under attack by several air raids. The Luftwaffe could easily identify Hull on the wide estuary of the River Humber as a location to attack, in contrast to some of the other northern cities. Therefore, aircraft crews on return flights to their bases frequently dropped their bombs on Hull. The two raids over the 7ᵗʰ – 9ᵗʰ of May, known as Hull's blitz, were the most concentrated and accurate of the entire war on the city, with a total of 277 tons of high explosives and around 30,000 incendiaries dropped. This resulted in major destruction of the city centre, as well as the adjacent dock area, with thousands of damaged houses, 420 people killed and 325 seriously injured. These attacks, in addition to the earlier air raids on Hull, especially two particularly heavy assaults in March, meant that it had now become a common sight to see large numbers of Hull residents trekking into the surrounding countryside, to spend the night away from the dangers of the air raids, before returning to the city in the morning.

On passing through the devastated city centre on his way home, Jack was shocked to see the extent of the damage. The large Co-Op store in Jameson Street, where his father was employed, was now just a ruined shell, as were half of the shops in the centre of the city. Meeting his sister Gwen after she finished work, he was relieved to hear that all the family were safe, although he was concerned about how close she had been to being caught up in it, as she relayed her tale. Gwen told Jack that she had been in the city centre near the Cecil Cinema, with a friend, when the sirens started. Everyone was directed into the shelter outside the Station Hotel. After several hours the all-clear was sounded and they emerged from the shelter. There was destruction everywhere, including the Co-Op store and the Cecil Cinema, which were both destroyed, as Jack had just witnessed. When Gwen had walked past the ruined Co-Op, she felt heartbroken to see the front of the whole block down, with glass and rubble right across the road. It was a struggle to make her way through the ruins. She then walked all the way home to tell their dad, Leonard. He immediately got on his old bike and cycled to his beloved shop, to see the wreckage for himself.

Gwen then told Jack that following the destruction of the Jameson Street store, Leonard was now working at another Co-Op, a furnishing shop with an attached warehouse, on Beverley Road. This shop was close to another cinema which had also been destroyed, The National Picture Theatre. Leonard was now fire-watching at his new shop on most nights. Jack was naturally concerned for his father being alone at night in that large, deserted building, even though Leonard had already dealt with three unexploded incendiaries that had landed in their garden at home, during an earlier raid.

After eight days in Hull, on the 2nd of June, the Kingswood was again ready for sea. The ship was to make a return journey north around Britain, back to Loch Ewe in Scotland, ready for its next Atlantic crossing. In the early hours of the morning, the day after Jack had left on the Kingswood, there was another air raid on Hull, this was the fiftieth. Leonard was fire-watching at his workplace when four highly explosive bombs landed close by. The nearest one came down in Margaret Street, just 300 feet away from him. Tragically, the all-clear siren had sounded, and people were making their way home from the shelters when the bombs dropped, resulting in 27 people killed and 11 seriously injured. Leonard gave assistance to some of the injured. Three weeks later, on the 22nd of June, Hitler ordered the invasion of Russia. This led to a reduction in the frequency and strength of German aircraft bombing raids on Britain, but they continued sporadically on Hull throughout the war. At least with the invasion of Russia, the fear of Britain being invaded was reduced.

Safely completing its Atlantic crossing, and steaming south along the American coast, the Kingswood arrived at the Island of Cuba, the largest island in the West Indies, which was a new destination for Jack. Cuba was neutral, but supportive of the Allies. The ship docked on the 10th of July at Manzanillo, a small port on the southeast of the country, in humid sweltering temperatures of over 90 degrees Fahrenheit. The Kingswood was slowly loaded with its return cargo of sacks of sugar and some barrels of molasses, which were in very short supply back home in Britain. The crew were delighted to be able to spend some time relaxing ashore in this rather faded Spanish colonial town, which was principally reliant on the surrounding sugar cane estates, tobacco crops, fish canning plants, and leather goods factories. The white sandy beaches and palm trees nearby were a world away from the war raging in the ocean beyond the island and back home in Britain. The small bars selling beer, rum and cigars, and the shops and cafes with their local dishes of spicy rice, beans and chicken, with plenty of fresh fruit, provided a welcome escape from work.

On the 14th of August, after completing the loading of her cargo in Cuba, the Kingswood sailed via Hampton Roads, Virginia in America to Halifax in Canada, to commence her return to Britain in the large Convoy HX.145. It took seven hours to assemble the ships into twelve columns, totalling 85 cargo vessels, 30 of which were carrying oil or petrol which were vital for the war effort. This convoy turned out to be the safest voyage that Jack had been on, and mid-way he was able to celebrate his 21st birthday with a cake made by the cook, and a box of cigars from his fellow officers. With no submarine attacks along their northerly route, and no aircraft attacks around the coastal waters of Britain (as the Germans' attention was focused on the Gulf of Finland and the Barents Sea with their on-going invasion of Russia), the Kingswood arrived safely at Dundee on the 3rd of September.

On arriving back home for a week's leave, Jack was relieved that his family was still safe, despite Hull having suffered several more air raids causing further damage to some houses in his street. His mother was delighted to report that she had caught a glimpse of the King and Queen on their visit three weeks earlier, to witness the bomb-damaged city. Just a couple of days into Jack's leave, the radio stations and newspapers reported the unsuccessful attack by a German submarine on the Greer, an American destroyer, near Iceland. This attack prompted President Roosevelt to escalate America's response to future threats, taking the country a step closer to direct involvement which was warmly welcomed by the crews of the Merchant Navy.

Jack returned to Dundee, for what would become his final voyage on the Kingswood. Dundee was home to the International 9th Submarine Flotilla, which comprised British submarines, along with crews and vessels from Poland, the Netherlands, France and Norway. Although the city of Dundee was a major producer of millions of sandbags from its jute mills, the cargo on the Kingswood was purely military. As the ship left port on the 15th of September, as part of operation Monsoon, its cargo consisted of more than twenty wooden crates of Hurricane planes, plus various types of vehicles, machinery and stores.

Having again steamed safely around Britain in a coastal convoy, on the 24th of September the Kingswood left Oban to join convoy OS.7 which had sailed from Liverpool. Along with 43 other cargo vessels, their destination was now confirmed as West Africa. Near the Azores, following instructions from naval authorities, the convoy successfully diverted around three U-Boats which had already sunk several ships just before they reached that area. Unfortunately, there was one attack which took place near the end of their voyage off the West African coast. The cargo vessel the Nailsea Manor was torpedoed after she dropped behind the main convoy but thankfully all her crew survived by rapidly abandoning ship. However, the ship itself, which was carrying 6,000 tons of military stores including 1,000 tons of ammunition and a landing craft in four sections, was sunk. The rest of the convoy arrived safely in Freetown, the capital of

Sierra Leone, on the 14th of October. Jack, along with the rest of the crew, remained on board the Kingswood in Freetown for three days. They subsequently joined several other ships to sail east along the coast for another 850 miles, to the port of Takoradi on the Gold Coast (Ghana).

In July 1940 Takoradi was chosen as the port to commence the huge transfer of aircraft to the key strategic location of R.A.F. Abu Sueir, 4,000 miles away. R.A.F. Abu Sueir was located close to the Suez Canal, 72 miles from Cairo. It was vital for Britain's war effort that the British had control of this area, and this transfer was given the name Operation Monsoon.

On arrival at the dockside of Takoradi, the crated Hurricane airplanes with the associated stores and machinery from the Kingswood, were quickly unloaded and driven to a nearby air base where they were assembled. From there they would fly in stages across Africa in small groups, stopping every few hundred miles for refuelling and maintenance at specific remote locations. They flew across tropical jungles, mountains, scrub land and barren desert plains, via larger bases at Lagos, Kano and Khartoum. Then they flew northwards following the River Nile, arriving at their destination of Abu Sueir in Egypt seven days later. Civilian aircraft would then return the pilots of the fighter aircraft back from Egypt to Takoradi, so the process could be continuously repeated. Beginning with the first flights from Takoradi in September 1940, during the next three years, over 5,000 planes were transferred by this method. Without this route, the ships with their precious cargoes of planes would have had to have made the 8,000-mile journey around South Africa to Egypt, which would have taken at least another five weeks, and in addition, they would have been at risk of being attacked en route.

Jack and the rest of the crew had been unaware of the final destination of their military supplies, yet they were to learn that their next cargo for the return journey was to be iron ore, for the steel industry of North East England. As a cargo, despite its weight, the iron ore took up a comparatively small amount of space within the ship, therefore any breach of its hull would cause sea water to pour inside within seconds and cause a fatal rapid sinking. Iron ore as cargo also tended to shift its position in the holds in severe weather, causing substantial rolling of the ship like a pendulum, making for an uncomfortable voyage.

Retracing the coastal journey 850 miles westwards, back to Freetown, hugging the coast due to increasing submarine activity with armed trawler escorts, the Kingswood then steamed slowly for three hours up the Sierra Leone River, with a pilot to navigate the narrow channel and mud flats. Arriving at the wharf at the port of Pepel, surrounded by jungle, large loading grabs deposited the grey iron ore powder into the holds, from the mountain of ore and bauxite extending to the river's edge. The iron ore powder had come by rail from the huge Marampa mines 50 miles inland. These mines had only opened in 1933 and produced one of the purest iron ores in the world, outside of Sweden.

By the 19th of November, the Kingswood was loaded and sitting in Freetown harbour with 32 other vessels, forming convoy SL.93 bound for Liverpool. Six other ships were also carrying iron ore, the remainder were carrying an assortment of vital raw materials including manganese, copper, potash, palm oil, gold, sugar, rubber, cottonseed, jute and linseed. Luck was again with Jack as they swept out wide into the Atlantic and were able to complete a trouble-free voyage back to Britain. They diverted to Oban, then travelled in a coastal convoy to Methil, finally reaching Middlesbrough where on the 17th of December 1941 they unloaded their cargo for the Teesside steelworks.

Following their safe trip, the news that America had declared war on Japan on the 8th of December, and on Germany on the 11th of December, was received with joy on board the Kingswood and brought the crew some hope for victory. Two days after arriving in Middlesbrough Jack left the ship for the last time. He had some leave due and was able to spend Christmas at home with his family. By another fortunate chance he would avoid having to sail on the Kingswood's next trip, which would be in an arctic convoy to Murmansk in Russia, in winter.

'The SS Kingswood' (the Constantine Group)

'Atlantic Convoy' (Alamy, colour by Grant Kemp)

'Derby House, Western Approaches Command Centre, Liverpool' (Author's photo)

'Derby House, Western Approaches Command Centre, Liverpool' (Author's photo)

'Hull Western Docks following air raid, May 1941' (Kew National Archives)

'Hull Western Docks following air raid, May 1941' (Kew National Archives)

'Hull Western Docks following air raid, May 1941' (Kew National Archives)

'Hull Eastern Docks following air raid, May 1941' (Kew National Archives)

'Hull Eastern Docks
following air raid,
May 1941'
(Kew National Archives)

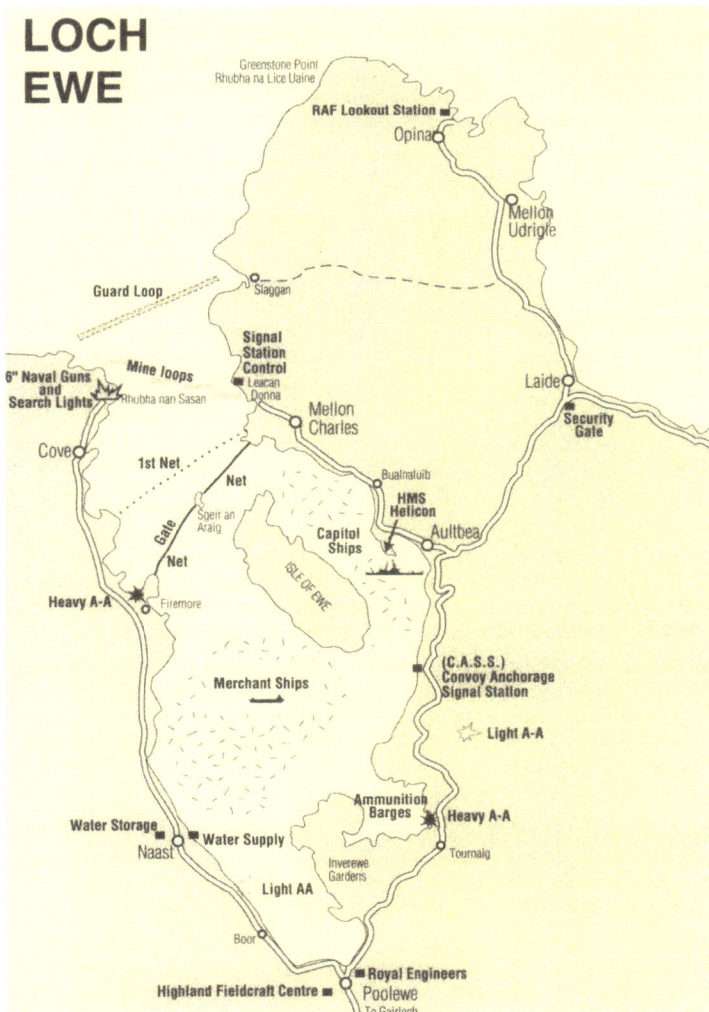

'Loch Ewe map, WW2'
(George Chadwick, Loch Ewe WW2)

'Unloading Hawker Hurricane plane at Takoradi' (I.W.M.)

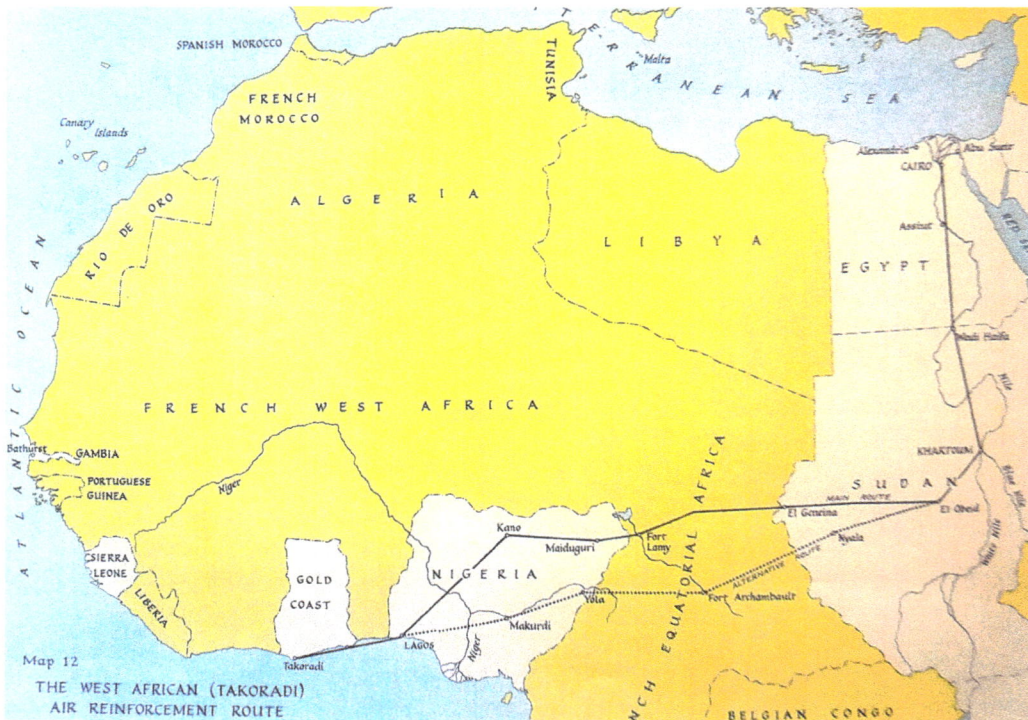

'Map showing flight route from Takoradi to Egypt' (Alamy)

Chapter 6
SS Holmbury

New Year's Eve 1941 was a cold blustery day in Teesside. Jack signed on with his next ship, the SS Holmbury, in what felt like a repetition of the beginning of his first trip as a radio officer back in September 1940. This was another well-worn tramp steamer, built in 1925 in Glasgow and would usually be carrying coal on outbound voyages, often to South America. The Holmbury was owned by Alexander Capper and Co Ltd, who at the start of the war had fourteen ships, each one ending with the suffix 'bury'. Tragically twelve of them had already been sunk.

The SS Holmbury was home for Jack for longer than any other ship during the war, so he became very attached to it while he was travelling to new countries and a new continent. The ship was reliable, with good crews, although there were only basic facilities on board. It was also his first time of working with two other radio officers, which meant his shifts would be four hours on and eight hours off, allowing him to have a much better sleep and rest pattern than before. These new hours also allowed Jack to assist the Captain with much of his paperwork and administration. Jack had prior experience of these from his earlier years of training as a purser before the war.

The crew of 45 men were mainly British but with two sailors from New Zealand. There was a gun crew of four, and five crew under the age of 18 years, who served as deck boys, pantry boys, cabin boys and mess boys. The first voyage followed the usual route via Methil, sailing around Scotland. They arrived at Oban to await convoy OG.79, then joined it at sea, on its way to Gibraltar. The Holmbury left the convoy to dock at Lisbon in Portugal on the 6th of February, where its cargo of coal was unloaded. The rest of the convoy travelled on, to reach the destination of Gibraltar the following day.

Portugal remained neutral during the war, with its government more closely aligned to the Axis powers, whilst its citizens tended to support the Allied cause and the longstanding 550-year-old alliance between Portugal and Britain. Therefore, Lisbon quickly became a hub of espionage and a safe haven for deposed monarchs, escaping Allied servicemen, and thousands of refugees from occupied countries - including numerous homeless Jews who were trying to reach Israel. Carefully balancing trade with both sides in the conflict to help to improve its economic growth, Portugal imported large quantities of coal from Britain, and Germany bought wolfram ore (tungsten) from Portugal, as this was vital for the production of their military equipment.

As soon as the Holmbury had arrived in this unique melting pot of Allied and Axis interests in Lisbon, a member of the British consulate appeared on board the Holmbury. He proceeded to warn the crew of the dangers of inadvertently providing enemy agents with information about shipping movements, as these details would be forwarded to the German naval authorities. He explained that women were often used in bars as decoys and were paid 50 escudos for each report of definite convoy movements or reports of past voyages. This was worth around three weeks' wages for lowly paid firemen, or two months' wages for the youngest cabin boy. Quite often these women were still young, even in their teens, and desperate for money. The crew were also told to beware of senior Portuguese shipping agents who were regarded as pro-Axis, and to avoid certain bars which were known to be owned by Germans. Unsurprisingly, once ashore some of the sailors overindulged on the cheap, local red wine. One of the crew returned with a damaged hand from a fight in a bar, and two others were fined a day's wages for being drunk on board.

Due to security concerns, the crew had not been informed of their next port of call. Leaving Lisbon, they headed southeast through the Straits of Gibraltar. On the 17th of February, much to Jack's surprise, he found they were entering the port of Melilla in the Mediterranean. Although Melilla is on the North African coast and borders Morocco, it was (and still is) an autonomous city of Spain, having been so since the late 15th century. No one was allowed on shore at Melilla because, as was the case in Portugal, there were a number of locals sympathetic to the German cause. These agents were known to inform their naval authorities of the presence of Allied ships in port, in order to pass on that information to the Axis submarines in the Mediterranean. The city had also been the staging ground for the military coup d'etat that started the Spanish civil war in 1936. Due to these potential dangers, to speed up the loading of the return cargo of iron ore from the nearby mines, it was lifted above the holds of the Holmbury in the rail wagons and tipped straight in. By the following night she had steamed back 137 miles to the safety of Gibraltar.

The Holmbury was assigned to Convoy HG.79 for its voyage back to Britain. This convoy comprised 29 merchant vessels and, unusually, 15 of the other merchant vessels were also carrying iron ore, showing how vital this was to the war effort. Six of the remaining vessels were carrying oranges, mostly the bitter Seville type, to turn into marmalade in Hartley's factory in Liverpool. The German intelligence service had bases on both sides of the Straits of Gibraltar, in Tangiers in Morocco and close by at Algeciras in Spain. This meant that Jack and the crew were concerned that convoy movements could be monitored easily, but they were impressed when they saw their escorts form up.

These escorts consisted of ten recently built anti-submarine corvettes (one of them, HMS Coreopsis, subsequently starred as the fictional Compass Rose in the 1953 film the Cruel Sea), plus two modern cargo ships, the Empire Heath and the Empire Morn. These two cargo ships, known as CAM ships (catapult aircraft merchantmen), had recently been fitted with rocket catapults on their bows, on which a Hawker Hurricane fighter was positioned. These CAM ships were used as a stopgap measure, until sufficient aircraft carriers were available for escort duties. The German Focke-Wulf Condor planes were a major threat to the Allies' convoys, both through direct attacks and by guiding their U-Boats towards Allied convoys. The British land-based aircraft were too far away to be of use in protecting the convoys, so the Allies relied on these modified ships for protection.

Trials of the CAM ships had started in the summer of 1941 and a total of 35 were introduced. Although aircraft were only launched from them eight times, they downed eight enemy planes during their two years of use and undoubtedly prevented further submarine attacks. Once launched, the pilot either had to make it to land or ditch in the sea near a ship to be rescued. The only fatality among those launched was from the Empire Morn. This occurred two months after the Empire Morn had escorted Jack's convoy. Supporting a convoy sailing to Russia, a pilot shot down an enemy bomber but after bailing out he suffered serious injuries, resulting in his death.

Departing Gibraltar on the 22nd of February, the convoy safely reached British waters without incident. Two weeks later, the Holmbury discharged its cargo for the steel mills at Port Talbot, Wales. The other ships carrying their cargoes of ore dispersed to other steel making areas in Barrow, Workington, Scotland, the Tyneside and Teesside. Jack then had an unexpected break due to repairs on the Holmbury, followed by a week's leave. After loading a cargo of coal in Cardiff Jack's next trip would take him to a new continent over 6,000 miles away, which was much favoured by the crew.

The war in the Atlantic had by now moved into a new phase, with an increase in British and Allied shipping losses, up from 878 ships lost in 1940 to 1,299 ships lost in 1941. During 1942 the number of Axis submarines operating at any one time in the Atlantic almost tripled to around 115. When the USA entered the war, the Germans responded with Operation Paukenschlag (Operation Drumbeat). At the beginning of 1942 the Germans attacked along the Eastern American coastline and a few months later around the Caribbean. This resulted in huge shipping losses due to a refusal by the American naval command to adopt a convoy system, plus a lack of blackouts on the coast and insufficient anti-submarine ships. With these Axis attacks to the east of America, there was a reduction in German submarine activity in the rest of the North Atlantic, which was welcomed by Jack.

The Holmbury left Cardiff docks on the 29th of March 1942 and headed north to join convoy OS.24 which left Liverpool on the 2nd of April. The rest of this convoy was bound for Freetown in Sierra Leone, West Africa, but the crew of the Holmbury were delighted to be told that their destination would be South America, with their first port of call being Rio De Janeiro. During the Holmbury's voyage two Allied ships had been sunk off the coast of Brazil by an Italian submarine. All other distress calls monitored in the radio room during this time were initiated far from their route around West Africa. After two weeks they broke off from the main convoy and sailed independently southwest to the Brazilian coast on the Equator. Brazil had cut off diplomatic relations with Germany in January 1942 but were still officially neutral. In August 1942 due to unrestricted Axis submarine attacks on merchant shipping causing the sinking of several Brazilian ships, Brazil joined the Allies.

There was a growing concern on board the Holmbury for one of the young 18-year-old deck hands, William Morgan from Cardiff. Not long after departing, the sailor had complained of severe headaches, fluctuating temperatures and sleeplessness. Confined to the sick room his situation gradually got worse despite being given medication, including small amounts of morphine. Following messages and advice over the radio from the convoy commander, it was suspected that William had meningitis. On arrival at Rio de Janeiro on the 1st of May, the port doctor came on board and advised that William should be taken immediately to hospital. Tragically, he died there four days later, and his funeral the following day was attended by the Captain, Jack and several other members of the crew. Jack had been helping Captain Lawson with his clerical duties and now he had the sad task of helping to collect William's personal effects. He typed up the inventory of William's personal property which was entered into the ship's logbook. His belongings were kept on board the Holmbury to be returned to Britain.

After unloading the cargo of coal, the Holmbury continued her voyage south for over 1,000 miles in almost perfect weather following the coastline of Brazil. The crew felt more relaxed as they knew that no submarines operated this far south and the German surface raiders were no longer in the vicinity. The Holmbury entered the Rio De La Plata, the 140-mile-wide mouth of the estuary separating Uruguay and Argentina. Steaming upriver, the crew were reminded of one of the earlier raids of the war. The Holmbury sailed near to the visible superstructure remains of the German battleship Admiral Graf Spee, which had been damaged by the British Navy. The Graf Spee was subsequently scuttled within sight of Montevideo in the northern channel in December 1939. Continuing up the dark brown waters of the River Parana for 190 miles, the Holmbury reached Rosario the third largest city in Argentina on the 17th of May. Rosario was also the largest port in the country, despite being inland, as the river is broad and deep up to this point. Rosario had been well developed to become the leading export port for the vast fertile Pampas area to the south. The Holmbury loaded its return cargo of grain and departed two days later. However the crew left without their chief cook, who had cut off the top of his thumb and needed hospital treatment. Their final stop would now be the capital Buenos Aires, in neutral Argentina. The crew were delighted to be spending some time in this vibrant city. There were no blackouts but instead they enjoyed brightly lit broad streets, abundant food and drink, and a pleasant temperature with little humidity.

As the crew tied up, they noticed to their surprise that there was a German cargo ship nearby, flying a swastika. Then the customs officials came on board; they removed all the breechblocks from the guns and sealed the ammunition magazines. All the crew were told to provide their signatures, then they were photographed and fingerprinted by two local officials before they were allowed ashore, where a policeman was always on patrol by the gangway. Finally, they were warned that the authorities would be very strict in dealing with deserters. A British embassy official and the shipping agent then spoke to the crew. The officials put up a list of bars and cafes to avoid that were run or owned by Germans. Often, these had innocent sounding names, such as the Australian, Texas, Honolulu or the Mickey Mouse bar. The crew were given maps of Buenos Aires and details of organisations that were run for the benefit of Allied seamen by the very active local British community, including the Missions to Seamen and the Apostleship of the Sea. The most popular organisation was the Liberty Inn which encouraged mixing of all ranks and was run by the larger-than-life Cockney woman known as Big Kitty.

Therefore, Jack and the rest of the crew were able to take advantage of free concerts and dances, cheaper food and drink, games such as billiards and darts, reading and writing rooms (with some reduced fees for sending telegrams back home), and a free weekly tour around the countryside, in an old-fashioned motor charabanc. All officers were given free membership to several local social and sporting clubs. They were able to meet crews from other ships and exchange experiences, as there were always between three and five Allied ships in port at any one time. Facilities were in place at the Victoria Sailors' Home, to provide accommodation for seamen waiting to join ships, for convalescent patients after being discharged from hospital and for shipwrecked crews. Two lucky sailors from the Holmbury entered a raffle organised by the British Community Council and won tickets to the biggest event in the city at that time. This was a friendly football match between Argentina and their main rivals Uruguay, held on the 25th of May. Argentina won 4-1, in front of a crowd of 61,000 at the River Plate Estadio Monumental (which had only been completed four years previously) in the northern neighbourhood of Belgrano. Their tickets were two of the 60 free tickets supplied for seamen that year by the

Argentine Football Association. The rest of the crew joined in the noisy celebrations and fireworks that evening amongst a packed crowd in the city centre.

The Holmbury was ready for departure on the 2nd of June, having replenished her stores and coal bunkers, and taken on some additional general cargo. A final parting gift from the British community, which they gave to all British vessels, was the provision of fresh fruit, condensed milk and vitamin tablets, all of which was much appreciated by the crew. Returning to the wartime blackouts and vigilance on board the vessel, they steamed independently northeast along the Brazilian coast for 4,000 miles, then across the Atlantic Ocean to Freetown in Sierra Leone. In the radio room on board the Holmbury, numerous reports came through of Allied vessels being attacked. However, these attacks were predominantly happening in the Caribbean Sea and Gulf of Mexico areas. The Holmbury was able to avoid two active Italian submarines near their route, by keeping to a diversion, following instructions from the naval authorities in Britain.

After safely reaching Freetown and taking on fuel, the Holmbury joined Convoy SL.114 along with 39 other merchant vessels, to complete the remaining 3,000 miles back to Britain. Although they did not encounter any enemy submarines on this route, Jack was particularly shocked to hear a distress call halfway through their voyage, coming from the ship Avila Star. This was a sister ship to the Arandora Star which he had served on at the start of the war, one of the well-known Luxury Five liners from the Blue Star Line. The Avila Star was continuing to operate as both a passenger liner and a refrigerated cargo vessel between South America and Britain, as it had done since the mid-1920s. Jack and some of the officers and crew from the Holmbury had recently enjoyed socialising with the crew of the Avila Star, when both ships were berthed in Buenos Aires at the same time. Jack had even been invited to spend an evening aboard the Avila, as he had a previous connection to the shipping line. The Avila Star had left South America after the Holmbury, but as they sailed at a faster speed than the Holmbury, they were now a day ahead of Jack's convoy and sailing independently. On the 6th of July, 90 miles east of the Azores, the Avila Star was torpedoed by U-201. Of the 196 crew and passengers on board, tragically 84 died. Although many people were rescued within a day, one lifeboat carrying 24 people disappeared completely. Another open lifeboat spent 20 days trying to reach Portugal, before being rescued, but ten of the forty occupants died in that boat, from injuries, dehydration and drinking seawater. Four men were subsequently awarded M.B.E.s for their courage and seamanship in the lifeboat, which Jack read about some months later. Jack's convoy continued to travel safely and reached its destination in Scotland. The Holmbury unloaded its cargo on the Clyde before making its way to Cardiff for maintenance. Jack had six days of leave from the 1st of August. He arrived back in Hull, having just missed an air raid that had happened that morning near the docks, killing 23 civilians. The war never seemed far away to Jack.

The relentless schedule of convoys of merchant ships continued unabated, to keep up with the desperately needed supplies for the country. Jack's next voyage began with a route similar to his previous journey and turned out to be his longest to date. Jack was happy to remain on this ship and had become a trusted member of Captain Lawson's crew. The Captain, like Jack, was also from Yorkshire and Jack enjoyed a good working relationship under him. Having loaded another cargo of coal, they left Cardiff on the 8th of August 1942 and joined Convoy OS.37. This convoy comprised 31 ships and was heading for Freetown, Sierra Leone and Takoradi, Ghana. Four ships carried 74 Hurricanes and 26 Beaufighters, which were en route to Egypt, and would arrive via overland air trail from West Africa. The Holmbury headed independently towards South America, as soon as they were past the Canary Islands. On the way they heard that Brazil had declared war on Germany and Italy, following the sinking of several Brazilian vessels, six of which were sunk during the Holmbury's voyage south.

The Holmbury arrived in Montevideo, the capital of neutral Uruguay, on the 13th of September, after five weeks at sea and having covered 7,000 miles. The crew were keen to have some time to relax at last in a safe environment and Jack looked forward to being able to celebrate his recent 22nd birthday in another new city. As had happened on their previous trip to Buenos Airies, on arrival at Montevideo, the crew were given details of the pro Axis places to avoid, including certain bars around the port area and La Scala dance hall which was run by two Germans. The crew was pleased to find out about another Liberty Club which was run by the ex-pat community and had catered for over 8,000 men during the last year. It was popular with British, American, Norwegian, Dutch and Greek seamen, offering cheaper drinks and refreshments than elsewhere. The Liberty Club provided a motor launch service to the shore and city at a reasonable cost. Jack and the rest of the crew took advantage of this as they were anchored in the bay while their cargo was being offloaded into lighters. For those sailors who did overindulge or get into trouble, the Liberty Club also ran a voluntary picket at the central police station, from 11pm to 7am, with agreement from the Chief of Police to return any offenders back on board their ships, to preserve the pro-British feelings in the country.

Shore leave was at the discretion of the Captain and most of the crew managed around half of their eight-day stay on shore exploring Montevideo. This city with its broad tree-lined boulevards, electric trams and array of Art Deco buildings had been built up during the previous decades of European immigration, with people coming predominantly from Spain, Portugal and Italy. Jack took advantage of one of the Sunday excursions provided by the British Patriotic Committee. They travelled in an elderly motor coach to the hills above the city where 60 years previously a British company had built the Montevideo Waterworks and reservoirs. Jack then enjoyed a meal at a local restaurant before going sightseeing along the beaches at the east of the city. The sailors welcomed the break from the nervous strain of weeks at sea and appreciated the huge traditional barbeques of roast lamb, with drinks, as an improvement on the basic food provided on board their ship or back home in Britain.

Their time in South America was extended as after their cargo had been unloaded, they steamed across the River Plate to spend two weeks in Buenos Aires where they loaded tinned beef and cereals. Then they commenced their long voyage back home to Britain but this time they went by a different route. Over the next three weeks the Holmbury steamed north around Brazil, then headed northwest, entering the Caribbean Sea. This was where several U-Boats were still on patrol, and they had sunk 15 British and American cargo ships during these last three weeks. Arriving at the tropical island of St. Lucia, the Holmbury dropped anchor at the small southern port of Vieux Fort. The Americans had built a landing strip and airfield at Vieux Fort, as part of the defences of the West Indies, and the crew mixed with some of American military personnel in the few rum shops and bars in the town. Many of the crew had already spent their wage advances in South America, so the main occupation, after their duties had been completed, was fishing in the idyllic blue sea, while appreciating the sunshine. They hung fishing lines over the sides of the ship and rowed the jolly boat amongst the locals who were in canoes. There was an abundance of fish including large tuna and barracuda, and they cooked the fish they had caught on makeshift barbeques on the beach. On days like this it was difficult to imagine there was a deadly war happening around them, but this would soon change.

With fresh provisions of vegetables and fruit on board (which without refrigeration, did not keep fresh for long), the Holmbury left St. Lucia to steam 200 miles to the Port of Spain in Trinidad, where it anchored for two nights. Then the Holmbury joined Convoy TAG.20 which initially consisted of thirteen merchant ships and six US navy escorts. The convoy steamed due west, following the coast of Venezuela for two days arrived and near the islands of Aruba and Curacao, which both had important oil refineries owned by the Royal Dutch Shell Company. The convoy was now 40 miles north of the Venezuelan coast, where they were joined by nine tankers and two Dutch escorts for the last leg of the voyage to Cuba. Unfortunately for the convoy, U-Boat 163 had spotted the formation of the merchant ships. This U-Boat had been able to operate around the West Indies for the last month by being supplied by a large German submarine known as a Milch Cow, enabling it to remain on station longer whilst far from its base in Bordeaux.

Just after 5.30pm on the 12th of November, the German submarine closed in and fired three torpedoes at the convoy. The lookouts on the lead escort, the American gunboat USS Erie, spotted water spray 2,000 yards away on the starboard side. Turning to investigate, they then noticed two torpedoes heading in their direction. Sounding the siren, they began turning to port, however one torpedo struck the ship on her starboard side, ripping a 45-feet wide hole below the waterline. The resulting explosion ruptured her oil tanks and set off massive fires that ignited the charges for the Erie's six-inch guns, killing seven men and injuring seventeen others. Meanwhile Jack and the rest of the crew of the Holmbury, less than half a mile away, were suddenly galvanised to respond. They rushed to action stations and put on their lifejackets while feeling the shock waves of the damaged escort, as the order to steam away at full speed was given. Further shock waves were felt on board the Holmbury as the convoy passed by the burning USS Erie. Four other escorts began depth charging where they thought the submarine might be, the crew wondering if another torpedo was heading towards them. Over the next twenty minutes, as the convoy gradually left the area, further explosions were heard from the burning escort ship. Two American aeroplanes, from their airfield on the island of Curacao, also joined in the search for the submarine.

After an hour, the USS Erie was able to manoeuvre its way to beach itself on the coast of Curacao, not far from the main harbour of Willemstad. Here, the Erie remained burning for several days. Although eventually the fires were put out, attempts to take her to port failed, and the following month she capsized and sank. After three more anxious days the convoy reached the safety of Guantanamo, a US naval base in Cuba, before heading to New York the following day in a larger convoy GN.20. They arrived on the 23rd of November 1942 at New York, which had become a major convoy formation area over the last year. The final stage of the return journey across the North Atlantic was beset with fierce winter storms. Fourteen of the 45 merchant vessels that left New York on the 25th of November had to return to ports in either Canada or America during the first week of the intended voyage, due to mechanical problems, failure to keep sufficient speed, or collisions. This did at least reduce the threat of being spotted by the waiting U-Boats, but Jack and the crew of the Holmbury were exhausted by the time they reached British waters. It had been an elongated trip of 80 days, coming back from Argentina, travelling over 10,000 miles. Finally, they arrived in Southampton on the 23rd of December 1942 and looked forward to some welcome leave.

Jack collected his rail warrant and the ration cards he needed for his period of leave. On Christmas Eve, Jack travelled on the packed trains back to Yorkshire with Captain Lawson, who lived in the fishing village of Robin Hood's Bay, 60 miles north of Hull. Jack's family was overjoyed to see him, especially as it was the Christmas period, and they were relieved that he had made it back home again safely. An added unexpected bonus was finding out that his friend Sam Burwell was also on leave. After serving in the Mediterranean, Sam was now enrolled at Battersea College in London, learning radar mechanics for the Royal Navy.

The pair of young seamen spent time together in their local, the Crown Inn, and swapped stories of their lucky escapes. Life had become increasingly difficult for people throughout Britain, as Jack and Sam witnessed in their families. During 1942 virtually everything in Britain that had not already been rationed was now included in the growing restrictions, including soap, sweets, biscuits, coal, gas and electricity. Even the meagre quantity of petrol ration ceased altogether during the year. The reason was quite simple - the Germans and their allies were winning the Battle of the Atlantic.

By December 1942, U-Boat numbers had risen to almost 400, which was a huge increase from 250 in January, and this was despite 86 Axis submarines being lost during the year. Worldwide losses in tonnage, due to destruction by Axis submarines, were higher in November 1942 than during any other month of the war, with 119 ships totalling 729,000 tons destroyed – mostly in the Atlantic. Although the Allies could now deploy 450 escort ships of all types, this was still not enough to go onto the offensive, and there remained a large area in the mid-Atlantic where there was no air cover. So grave was the situation that in November the Prime Minister, Winston Churchill, had formed a Cabinet Anti-U-Boat Warfare Committee to try to reverse the situation, as an urgent priority. The conclusion of the battle for the Atlantic would however be resolved in the summer of the following year, 1943, as Jack and the crew of the Holmbury would discover.

'The Holmbury at Gibraltar, 7th February 1942, Jack second from the right'
(Author's photo, colour Grant Kemp)

'C.A.M. ship at Greenock 1942, testing a Hawker Sea Hurricane aircraft'
(Alamy, colour Grant Kemp)

'List of belongings of William Morgan, compiled by Jack' (Kew National Archives)

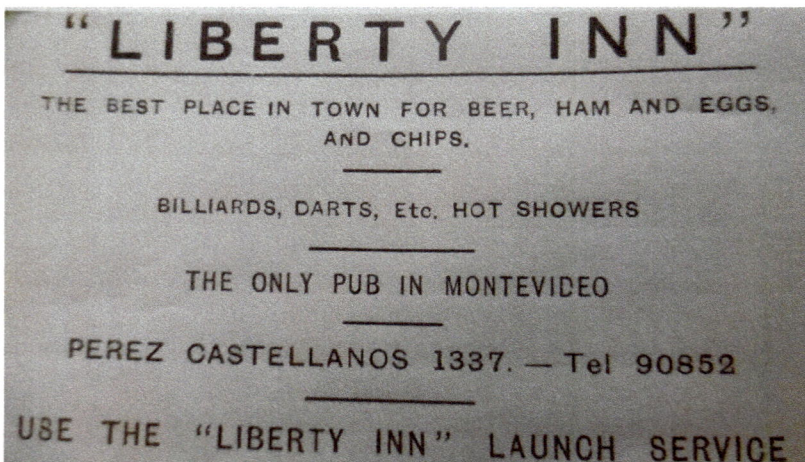

'Flyer for Liberty Inn, Montevideo' (Author's)

'Avila Star sunk, 6th July 1942' (Tuck postcard, author's)

'USS Erie burning on the beach on the Dutch Island of Curacao off the coast of Venezuela, days after being torpedoed on 12th November 1942' (Alamy, colour Grant Kemp)

'Map of North and South America convoy routes' (Alamy)

Chapter 7
SS Holmbury's Final Voyage

Just before eight o'clock on the morning of Wednesday the 5th of May 1943, Jack was on the bridge of the Holmbury, with Captain Lawson and a few of the other officers and crew. They were steaming independently just north of the equator on their return voyage from South America to Freetown, Sierra Leone, to join a convoy for the final leg back to Britain.

It had been another successful trip to Montevideo in Uruguay to unload their cargo of coal, and to Buenos Aires in Argentina where they loaded a cargo of tinned meat. They returned to Montevideo to load up linseed and leather hides, before leaving on the 17th of April. The weather had been kind to them, but three days beforehand they had received a warning from the British Naval authorities. They were told to divert their course southwards towards the nearest mainland, which was Liberia, then steam northwest following the coast to Freetown in Sierra Leone. They expected to complete the remaining hundred miles and arrive at port that evening.

With the rhythmic thudding sound of the ship's engines pushing them through the calm sea at nine knots, the crew were in good spirits. Jack and the others on the bridge laughed at the sight of two of the deckhands chasing a rat on the deck below them. It was likely that it was one of several vermin which had emerged from the hold, hidden within their cargo of cattle hides. As the first mate and some of the crew headed down to the mess for breakfast, Jack went to begin his four-hour radio shift at 8am, relieving the third radio officer whose shift was ending. The crew were unaware that their ship had already been spotted, more than two hours earlier, by the German U-Boat 123, which had now manoeuvred ahead, and dived to commence its attacking run.

The captain of this submarine was Horst Von Schroeter, who was only 23 years old, just one year older than Jack, and on his second patrol. He had already gained a wealth of experience having served on this submarine as Watch Officer, under the decorated Captain Reinhard Hardegen. This was one of the first submarines operating off the coast of America in the first half of 1942, in Operation Drumbeat. In March 1943 U-Boat 123 had left the Lorient submarine base in Brittany, France, to patrol off the West African coast, but Horst's first attack on the 8th of April 1943 did not go to plan, as they attacked the neutral Spanish ship Castillo Montealegre and sunk it. This mistake was kept under secret orders, and the information was initially withheld. Ten days later Horst and his crew successfully sank the British submarine P-615 whilst it was on the surface. Within an hour they had also sunk the British cargo ship the Empire Bruce, followed some days later, by sinking the Swedish merchant vessel the Nanking on the 29th of April.

From ten feet underneath the waves, the crew on U-Boat 123 carried out a final check by periscope on the latest bearing, distance and speed of the target. They closed in on the

Holmbury. Horst ordered the firing of one torpedo which needed to travel just over 1,500 metres to be successful. After 101 seconds the jubilant crew were told that they had successfully struck the centre of the vessel. Meanwhile, on board the Holmbury, none of the lookouts had noticed the torpedo tracking towards them. At 8.40am there was a loud explosion on the port side in the thwartship bunker hold, which ran across the width of the ship behind the bridge. A large column of water was thrown up and onto the ship, the decks on either side of the hold buckled upwards, the engines stopped immediately, and steam poured out from inside due to the pipes being fractured. As there was only a wooden bulkhead between the bunker that had been hit and the adjoining number two hold (which was the largest on the ship at 70 feet long), water rapidly entered. To make matters worse, the watertight door between the coal bunker and the stokehold was open at the time, as the firemen were moving the coal. Consequentially, the stokehold, engine room and tunnel were rapidly flooded. The amount of water entering the ship caused it to settle swiftly, several feet lower in the sea. Tragically two of the firemen who had been working there, Joseph Borg (23) and John Attard (29) who were two of the nine Maltese firemen working in the depths of the ship, were killed almost immediately.

After the initial blast and recovering their senses, the first mate Percy Bedford and the other officers, who already finished their breakfast in the saloon, rushed back to their stations. Water had quickly flooded the saloon to two feet deep and more water was pouring in through the ventilators. Steam and smoke started to billow through the ship, adding to the confusion. In the radio cabin when the explosion had caused a huge jolt, Jack had managed to remain seated by grabbing the table. Trying to ignore the general shouts and confused noises, Jack spoke on the voice pipe to Captain Lawson, who gave him their latest position. They were 4-30 degrees North and 10-20 degrees West, approximately 80 miles from the Liberian coast of West African. Jack's training automatically kicked in, as he repeatedly sent out the distress call with their position and awaited a response.

Within five minutes of being hit, the Captain gave the order to abandon ship. However, even before the order to abandon ship was given, the four naval and two army gunners jumped straight over the side, which did not impress the rest of the crew! On both sides of the Holmbury there was a lifeboat, each 24-feet long with capacity for 32 people, and a jolly boat, each 17-feet long with capacity for 14 people. Jolly boats were generally used in port for ferrying people between ship and shore. Unfortunately, the explosion destroyed the port side jolly boat completely, and the blast unhooked the falls of the port side lifeboat, causing it to plunge into the water and become waterlogged. There were also two sets of canvas Carley rafts which were stacked three high on a pair of rails at each side of the ship. These could easily be cut loose to drop straight into the sea. Some of the crew quickly freed the rafts and jumped over the side into them. Two of the firemen then tried to lower the starboard lifeboat but accidentally let go of the falls and the boat tumbled into the sea. The starboard jolly boat was also launched, but it floated away from the ship's side.

Most of the crew were now in a raft or in the sea trying to retrieve and then bail out the starboard lifeboat. There were just five people left on board - Captain Lawson, the first mate, Jack and two other crew. Jack collected all the confidential and wireless books, placed them in a weighted box and threw them overboard. Twenty minutes after being hit these last remaining crew members went to the side of the ship - which was now so low in the water that they could step over the rail - and clambered into the last remaining raft. As Jack left the ship, he noticed several rats running around the deck and immediately thought of the saying 'like rats fleeing a sinking ship'. He was at least relieved that unlike his two previous sinkings, this was happening in daylight and the sea was relatively calm.

The five men in their raft rowed over to the adrift starboard jolly boat and climbed in. The German submarine broke surface nearby and almost immediately they saw three men run to the forward mounted gun. Realising that the Holmbury which they were still very close to was about to be fired on, they started to row towards the rest of their crew in their lifeboat and rafts. Within a few minutes, the firing from the submarine commenced and the crew in the boats watched as a total of 26 shells exploded along the Holmbury. Ever-increasing amounts of smoke and flames appeared, until finally the vessel turned over on its starboard side and sank, sending a final large column of water gushing into the air.

It was a sad sight for Jack to witness the Holmbury, which had been his home at sea for the past 16 months, being destroyed in front of him. But now his thoughts turned to survival. After the Holmbury had disappeared, the U-Boat slowly started to glide across the water, heading in their direction. Captain Lawson had removed his jacket so he could not be identified. He told Jack and the other crew that if they were questioned, they were to say that their captain was believed to be dead - which they did when the U-Boat came alongside. The submarine then moved to where the rest of the crew were, a short distance away in their lifeboat and rafts. Some of the other officers had removed their badges of rank, not wanting to be taken prisoner. After questioning them to no avail, Horst Von Schroeter soon returned his submarine to Jack's jolly boat. Towering above them in the conning tower, Captain Von Schroter, speaking in clear English, again demanded to know who the captain was, but he was greeted with silence. After he had climbed down to the submarine's deck and was level with the jolly boat, he questioned each of the crew without success. Finally, he stared at Captain Lawson and said in clear English, 'You are the captain, please come on my submarine.'

As the Captain left the small boat to climb aboard the large submarine, he whispered good luck to Jack and then asked Jack to let his wife know what had happened. Jack would not see his Captain again until after the end of the war. While all this was happening, one of the German crew was taking photographs and six others were continually scanning the sky with binoculars, wary of any aircraft appearing. Then the submarine moved away, until it was eventually out of sight.

The time was now just after 10am, an hour and a half since the Holmbury had been hit. Some of the survivors of the Holmbury picked up one final member of their crew who was clinging to a piece of wreckage and then they all gathered together to decide on their course of action. Unsurprisingly, there was some disagreement about whether to stay put or head to land 80 miles away and then to add more complexity to the dispute, someone reported that he had seen a shark earlier. In addition, one of the lifeboats required regular bailing out, as when it had fallen from the Holmbury into the sea the hull had been damaged, although the boat remained seaworthy. The hole had been patched up by the second mate Arthur Clayton, who was an experienced officer, using some clothes. Arthur had raced in the sailing trials for the German 1936 Olympics, and he was firmly of the opinion that they should head for land, in the three separate boats. However, another officer wanted them to tie all three boats together with ropes, but Arthur knew it would be impossible to sail far with three boats attached to each other. After spending some time arguing about the different options, the men collected all the emergency provisions and gear and shared it out between the three boats. Then with some of the crew in each of the three boats they all set sail to the northeast, heading for the nearest African coastline.

Within a short space of time, as Arthur had predicted, it became impossible to sail with the three boats attached together, so the men rearranged themselves and their provisions, into just the two lifeboats and set sail again, making slow but steady progress in the light winds. During the afternoon, an America aircraft from the base at Roberts Field near Monrovia, the capital of Liberia, appeared overhead. The aircraft dropped food and water to them, plus a portable emergency wireless which considerably lightened the mood within the boats.

Overnight, the sky became overcast with occasional rain showers and there was some lightning in the distance. With the lower temperatures the blankets on board the lifeboats were very welcome and much needed, especially for several of the crew who had only been in shorts when they abandoned ship. Many of the men felt overwhelmed by the sheer expanse of the ocean, which was surrounding their small boats, especially as they were without their Captain. However, unbeknown to them he was not that far away. During the following morning of Thursday the 6th of May, U-123 was patrolling in the same area that the Holmbury crew were sailing in their lifeboats. On board the submarine, Captain Horst Von Schroeter called Captain Lawson to the periscope at noon. Captain Lawson could see his crew in their lifeboats under sail, which brought him some relief. The lifeboats had made steady progress and were now only about 20 miles off the coast of West Africa. That evening, sometime after dusk had fallen at around 7pm, the men in their lifeboats heard the heavy crashing of waves and realised that they were too close to shore, as it would be unsafe to try to land in the darkness. They manoeuvred back offshore and decided it would be safer to try to land the following morning in daylight. Both boats subsequently deployed their sea anchors to maintain their position and the men spent another frustrating, cramped, uncomfortable night in the lifeboats, the rain adding to their discomfort.

After daybreak on the 7th of May, with the coastal jungle in full sight and the wind dropping during the night, the crew on the two lifeboats used their oars to make some headway against the strong current. They tried to row towards what appeared to be a small lagoon, but as they rowed closer, they could see that there was a heavy surf which could potentially swamp their boats. As they paused to decide whether to proceed or instead to try to reach land further along the coast, several canoes appeared with natives paddling towards them. The Holmbury survivors were unsure whether or not the locals were friendly, but soon the crew realised that the natives had come to help them. With a smattering of English, the locals informed the crew that they would take them ashore two at a time on each of their canoes, as due to the dangerous swell the canoes would be a safer way to get ashore than rowing the lifeboats.

Two by two, the crew squeezed into the wooden canoes and had a thrilling ride through the foaming surf before being landed on a sand bar by the beach, now feeling in high spirits in contrast to how they felt during their challenging journey. Jack was safely on land when Arthur, the second mate, arrived on another canoe. Arthur approached one the other officers who had arrived on the beach before him, doffed his hat and pronounced, 'Doctor Livingstone I presume.' The relief was immense for all the crew. As they excitedly congregated together, another American plane passed overhead and dropped a message advising them to walk 15 miles northwards to a settlement for help. First, the natives guided the crew to their small village near the beach where they were given water and fruit for their journey. As several of the crew had no shoes, they started to rip up the blankets they had brought with them from the lifeboats to try to make some kind of protective footwear for the long walk ahead. The native women stopped them and quickly crafted native-style sandals for them. These proved to be very comfortable and practical for their journey, and the women were delighted to keep the blankets in exchange.

The chief radio officer sent out a message on the portable transmitter, but it was never acknowledged. At about 1pm the crew waved goodbye to the villagers and began their trek along the coast in the tropical temperatures and high humidity. It became a gruelling walk, especially for those with injuries. The men frequently had to leave the sandy beaches when the route became too rocky, and hike inland through patches of jungle. Monkeys and birds noisily screeched in the trees surrounding them. Added to this, the men had to be constantly alert for snakes or crocodiles when they crossed over several muddy rivers and a swampy marsh area.

Finally, after seven hours, tired and sweating, they reached their destination. Arriving in darkness they came across a small coastal village consisting of fewer than 40 people, in Grand Bassa County. They were greeted enthusiastically by the natives, who immediately started cooking for them. Some of the men were suffering from cuts and burns. Jack was in charge of the two first aid kits which they had brought with them from the lifeboats, so he asked the men to line up for treatment. Thinking that he was nearing the end of the queue, he turned and was surprised to find that the queue was almost as long as it had been initially, as some of the locals also wanted treatment. With only a basic first aid course to his name, he applied the limited creams, plasters and bandages that he had. The natives were so delighted that they collected and handed out, coconuts and fruits, such as pineapples, bananas, oranges and mangoes, all of which were virtually unavailable in Britain during the war. Despite having barely any English, the natives ushered Jack and the crew, a few at a time, into the headman's hut to wash and clean themselves. They were invited to sit in a circle on the ground with a fire burning at the centre of the circle, as the food was now ready for them to enjoy. There was a huge pot of fish and chicken soup to share, plus parcels of large leaves wrapped around cassava chips. This was all gladly eaten with gusto by the crew who had only had basic cold survival rations for the last few days.

Delighted to see their guests finishing all the food, the natives then entertained the sailors with ceremonial dances and songs, backed by a constant rhythm of tom-toms beating, while the crew clapped along enthusiastically. The crew then felt that it was time for them to provide some entertainment. A group of them jumped up and started performing the Palais Glide dance by linking arms in two rows, just as they did in the Mecca dancehalls back home. The villagers thought this dancing was amusing and joined in with the steps, to laughter all around. With the continuing beating of the tom-toms the entire 43 members of crew then started singing and dancing the popular wartime song by Ivor Kirchin and his band from 1938, 'The Chestnut Tree.' This catchy tune had everyone shouting the song while they performed the accompanying movements. With their arms swaying and their bodies bending, they hopped and stamped their feet. It was the most bizarre and hilarious sight that Jack saw during the war. There followed a final couple of renditions of another popular British wartime song, 'Roll Out the Barrel.' In great spirits, they all eventually found a space to sleep in some of the huts vacated for them by the villagers. As the embers of the fire slowly burnt away, the ocean stretched out in front of them, the jungle was close by on both sides and behind them, and the sailors witnessed the mass of stars in the vast dark sky above.

The next day Jack received an urgent request from the headman to go to his hut immediately as his wife needed attention. Jack's heart sank as he was worried by what might be required, when he only had basic first aid knowledge. He took a married gunner along for support and presented himself rather timidly at the door of the hut. His fears were soon allayed when he saw that an ingrowing toenail was the trouble. Thankfully, he was able to deal with this condition, much to the delight of the headman and his wife.

The next day a sailing yacht arrived, owned by an American. Several of the crew boarded and were taken up the coast around 75 miles to Monrovia, the capital of Liberia, where there was a strong American military presence. Jack and the remainder of the crew enjoyed another day relaxing with the villagers and swimming in the nearby lagoon. Then they tried to make themselves useful by collecting wood for cooking, and a couple of them went fishing with the native men in their canoes. The village headman invited the sailors who were still in their village to another meal that evening. The crew were surprised to find one table was laid with six cups, saucers and plates, all rather old and chipped. More delicious food adorned the table and was gratefully eaten by the crew. The chief was overjoyed to be able to eat with his guests in the manner that was according to their customs, and at the same time display his valuable treasures, the crockery.

This unique and tranquil experience ended the following day when an American invasion barge arrived at the beach to begin taking the sailors on the first stage of their journey home. The villagers waved them goodbye, and the crew were ferried to the capital, Monrovia, along the coast. Here, the British Council provided them with temporary accommodation, and they met up with the rest of their crew. After three days the whole crew was transferred again, this time by an armed Royal Navy trawler. It took an uncomfortable 24 hours to cover the 250-mile journey to Freetown, the main British port in West Africa. When they arrived on the 14th of May, most of the crew were billeted in a local grammar school, whilst Jack and the nine other officers were given rooms at the Grand Hotel in the centre of the city. The hotel was very close to the famous historical Cotton Tree, which was more than 300 years old, over 200 feet high and almost 50 feet wide. The Cotton Tree, which is actually a kapok tree, was reputed to be the place where newly freed slaves had offered prayers of thanks for their freedom, towards the end of the 18th Century.

May was the beginning of the monsoon period and almost every afternoon huge downpours of rain flooded the streets. The accompanying elevated temperatures and high humidity meant that Jack was keen to get home. The city's population had expanded enormously during the war as the docks grew in importance along with other British military units. Much of the infrastructure could not cope, resulting in open sewers, unmade roads and large shanty towns. There were numerous beggars and dogs scavenging everywhere. Although the crew had been given quinine tablets every day since arriving in Monrovia, some of them had contracted malaria which was rife in West Africa, and they were confined to their beds.

Much to Jack's relief, after eleven days of being in Freetown, they were finally told to report on board the troopship SS Orduna. This ship had been built in 1914 as a passenger liner but was now in a rather dilapidated state, having been in constant use as a troopship, particularly around Africa. Its peacetime passenger capacity was around one thousand people, but this was far exceeded in its war time role, with numerous hammocks slung from ceiling hooks throughout the ship. Jack and his fellow crew were pleased to see that they had been given basic bunkbeds, crammed into previous private bedrooms. They were joined by several other survivors from sunken merchant ships, who were also returning to Britain. There were five members of the Swedish merchant vessel SS Nanking, which had been torpedoed five days before the Holmbury.

Amazingly these survivors had also landed in a similar location in the Bassa area of Sierra Leone and eventually also arrived at Freetown. What none of them knew at the time was that it was the same U-Boat 123 that had sunk both ships.

The next few days in port were quite chaotic. First, more than 170 lascars (a name to describe sailors from the Indian subcontinent, SE Asia and the Arab world) embarked. Two days later they were disembarked. Next, some Italian P.O.W.s with their guards who had all been on board were disembarked, then subsequently re-boarded. Tragically, one of the civilian passengers on board suddenly died and his body was taken ashore.

Finally, the SS Orduna departed Freetown independently on the 4th of June, and called in briefly at Dakar, to pick up some more passengers. Then the ship steamed north to Casablanca in Morocco, arriving on the 14th of June where they stayed for two days. Another large group of Italian P.O.W.s (who had been captured during the recent defeat of Axis forces in North Africa) boarded with their guards. There was now a total of 1,501 prisoners with 816 guards on the packed ship. For most of Jack's colleagues the voyage became even worse. Seven of them became unwell with a bout of malaria, with only Jack, the second mate and the third engineer avoiding the illness. Arriving at Gibraltar, Jack was glad to get a pass to go on shore and he was pleased to be able to get off the cramped ship for a short while, to stretch his legs and have a drink. On the 22nd of June they left Gibraltar in high spirits because the southern shores of the Mediterranean were finally under Allied control. The Orduna travelled in a slow convoy with another packed troopship and three cargo liners. Much to everyone's relief they arrived safely back in Liverpool. Jack said farewell to his colleagues at midday on the 29th of June and arrived back home in Hull that evening with another extraordinary tale to tell.

The following day, Jack reported at the Marconi office in Hull. It was almost eight weeks since the Holmbury had been sunk and Jack was given an additional week's leave to be added to his accrued time off, which meant he had a total of four weeks' rest. Like most seamen, he was annoyed that the additional special war allowance for Merchant Sailors, which was now an extra £8 a month, had stopped when his vessel had sunk, which left him £16 short of what he might have earned. Although air raids had reduced considerably, the week before he arrived back in Hull 28 civilians had been killed and approximately a thousand homes damaged during the night of the 23rd – 24th of June. In the early hours of the morning of the 14th of July, Jack and the family were again sheltering under their stairs when another raid caused extensive damage in the city, killing 26 people.

One thing that Jack was determined to do was to fulfil Captain Lawson's last words to him in the lifeboat, to inform Lawson's wife about what happened to him. Knowing where she lived with her two young children in Robin Hood's Bay, about 60 miles away, he wrote to her with all the details, reassuring Lawson's wife that her husband was in good health when he was taken prisoner. Jack was then delighted to hear back from her, just as his leave was ending. She had recently been informed by the authorities that her husband was safe and now a prisoner in Germany.

For Captain John Bryce Lawson it had proved to be a harrowing experience once he was taken on board the submarine. After the U-Boat had moved away from the site of the sinking Holmbury, Lawson was searched, then given a change of clothes, some cigarettes and a glass of brandy which he appreciated. His bed was a hammock in the bow torpedo room, and the crew appeared young, tanned and friendly. On the third day, John Lawson confessed to the

Commander, Horst Von Schroeder, that he was in fact the Captain of the Holmbury. Schroeder wagged his finger and with a grin said,

"Do you think I did not know? I always pick the man who looks most worried."

Horst then informed his crew that the prisoner was the Captain of a ship, so he was to be treated with the respect his position commanded.

There followed a brief interrogation in the Commander's cabin, where John Lawson gave just enough information to appear helpful, but nothing that would not already be common knowledge, whilst also adding a few white lies. He verified his personal details, that he was married with a small son and daughter and came from Yorkshire. He confirmed that he had been a Captain for eight years, and the Holmbury had been en route from Argentina to Freetown. He stated that he had been on his first trip to South America, in contrast to the reality, which was that he had already completed several such trips. He explained that the voyage in peacetime took 28 days, but now during the war, it took six weeks, whereas the truth was that it was a voyage of 5 weeks. He was economical with the truth when he said that there had been three radio officers and two army gunners on board - and he failed to mention the four navy gunners who had also been on board. Regarding the radio equipment that had been on the Holmbury, Lawson admitted that there was a longwave radio transmitter of 200 to 1,000 metres and a shortwave transmitter receiver of 13 metres and upwards. Then he said that he did not know the manufacturer of the radio equipment, although he was well aware that it was made by Marconi. On being questioned about the general state of the war, Captain Lawson declared that there was sufficient food in Britain, although it was rationed. Lawson asserted that Americans were not disciplined in driving the convoys, calling them 'armchair sailors,' and in addition, the French dockworkers during peacetime were not very efficient. With regards to the war in the Atlantic he believed that the Allies were building faster than the Axis could destroy them, and starving Britain was impossible.

On the night of his fourth day aboard the submarine, the 8th of May, Captain Lawson was allowed onto the conning tower, where he joined four lookouts and the second officer. As the U-Boat continued to patrol on the surface along the West African coast while charging its batteries, Lawson was grateful to feel the fresh air on his face whilst hoping to learn something of value about the U-Boat's operation. Just after midnight, one of the lookouts pointed to something and handed his binoculars to the officer. After checking a faint shape on the horizon, he pressed an electric bell and immediately Von Schroeder ascended whilst the rest of the crew went to battle stations. After Von Schroeder made his own observations through the binoculars, he allowed Captain Lawson a brief look through them. It was obvious to them both that what they could see was an Allied merchant vessel showing no lights, because a neutral vessel would have all its lights on for safety reasons. Turning to Captain Lawson, the commander asked him to go below as they were submerging to conning tower depth to stalk the Allied ship, adding that it would not be pleasant for him to watch.

Lawson felt the U-Boat settle in the water and heard the diesel engines throb as it closed in for the kill. Four members of the crew then loaded two torpedo tubes. As Lawson settled in his hammock, his stomach was in knots. From far off he heard the commander order, "Fire!" and the bow of the U-Boat lifted as the torpedoes hissed away. Sixty-five seconds later Lawson gasped at the two distant muffled explosions, then there was silence for half a minute, until Von Schroeter spoke two final words of triumph, "Schiff gesunken!"

The ship that had been hit was the SS Kanbe, a recently built merchant vessel from Glasgow carrying 3,500 tons of copper. The ship had become separated from convoy TS.38 along the West African coast, heading from Takoradi to Freetown. Both torpedoes had exploded in the forward holds. Due to the weight of her cargo, she went down by the bows in two minutes, resulting in 66 deaths. Just five Indian crewmen managed to survive, and they were fortunate to be rescued fifteen hours later.

Captain Lawson felt totally helpless as the U-Boat continued its voyage. He realised that they were heading west, out into the mid-Atlantic, because for a large part of the time they were on the surface where the submarine could cruise at a faster speed. At least fresh air was now flowing through the submarine. The reason for the change of direction was that they were running short of fuel and a rendezvous had been arranged with a supply submarine. On the afternoon of the 18th of May, three star shells of green, red and white were fired into the air from the conning tower, as a recognition signal for the supply submarine in the pre-arranged location. Shortly afterwards the huge submarine U-460 appeared on the horizon. Being over two metres higher than conventional U-Boats, and carrying no torpedoes or deck guns, it was built purely as a floating supply base. Over the three hours they were together, U-123 was supplied with much needed fuel and some additional provisions. However, Captain Lawson was confined to his bed for security reasons.

The days passed slowly for John Lawson, and he realised they were heading north, passing the Azores. Although a week later the submarine crash-dived on sighting another merchant vessel, to his relief this was identified as a neutral Spanish ship, and it was allowed to pass. On the 30th of May, off the coast of Northwest Africa, the crew was in good spirits while celebrating the third anniversary of the submarine, but John Lawson did not join in and kept his thoughts to himself. Apart from some more practice dives, the rest of the voyage passed quietly. Extra lookouts were assigned, and the crew wore their lifejackets when on lookout duties, so Lawson knew they were coming near to the submarine's base at Lorient in France.

Finally at 6.30pm on the 8th of June the submarine tied up at her dock with the crew lined up on the deck, while a German band played to welcome them home. Von Schroeder turned to Captain Lawson and asked if there was anything he wanted before he went into captivity, and he replied, "Just a bottle of beer." He drank the beer, then ten minutes later he was escorted down the gangway. As Lawson passed the conning tower Von Schroeder beckoned him again and said,

"I had photographs taken of the sinking of your ship. You shall have them one year after the war has ended."

Captain Lawson thanked him, and he was then sent through occupied Northern Europe, travelling on a series of trains, to be processed and interned at Milag Nord Camp, 19 miles northeast of Breman in Germany. Here Lawson remained with several thousand other Allied merchant sailors, until they were liberated by the British Army at the end of April 1945, by which time his hair had turned completely white. Two years later, once he had been released from captivity, he received the photos of the sinking, as promised by Von Schroeder.

'The Holmbury settling low in the water after being hit by a torpedo on the morning of 5th May 1943' (Author's photos, colour Grant Kemp)

'Crew of U-123 firing 26 shells into the Holmbury to sink her'
(Author's photo, colour Grant Kemp)

'The jolly boat alongside U-123. Jack is rowing in the bow, with Captain Lawson two in
front of him on the starboard side' (Author's photo, colour Grant Kemp)

'Captain Lawson when just taken on board U-123 as a prisoner'
(Author's photo, colour Grant Kemp)

'Captain Horst Von Schroeter of U-123' (Author's photo, colour Grant Kemp)

'Crew and torpedo tubes inside U-123' (Author's photos, colour Grant Kemp)

'Arthur Clayton,
2ND Mate'
(Stuart Clayton,
colour
Grant Kemp)

'Jack back in Hull,
July 1943'
(Author's, colour
Grant Kemp)

'Map of sinking of Holmbury'
(Author's)

ALEXANDER SHIPPING CO. LTD.

April. 19 43

S.S. "Holmbury,"

State Name of Dock.
Best Postal Address.
Nearest Telegraph Office.
Port of   At Sea.

To whom it may concern.

This is to certify that Jack W. Stringer has served as 2nd Radio Officer in above vessel under my command from Dec. 1941 to above date.

During this period he has conducted himself in a strictly sober manner, at all times willing, and attentive to his various duties.

Owing to Mr Stringer's knowledge of clerical and accountant duties he was of great assistance to me in my work, acting as purser during the whole of his service.

I can therefore recommend him to anyone requiring his services, as a reliable officer, trustworthy and dependable, and I wish him every success in his future career.

J. B. Lawson.
Master.

'Reference for Jack written on board the Holmbury, two weeks before sinking' (Author's)

REGISTERED OFFICE: MARCONI OFFICES, ELECTRA HOUSE,
VICTORIA EMBANKMENT, LONDON, W.C.2.
TELEGRAMS: THULIUM, ESTRAND, LONDON.
TELEPHONE: TEMPLE BAR 4321 (ALL BRANCH EX)

The Marconi International Marine Communication
Company Limited
Marcont House, Chelmsford.

TELEPHONE: CHELMSFORD 3221.
TELEGRAMS: THULIUM CHELMSFORD
CODES: MARCONI INTERNATIONAL ETC

ALL COMMUNICATIONS
TO BE ADDRESSED TO
THE MANAGING DIRECTOR
THE REFERENCE AND DATE OF
THIS LETTER BEING QUOTED

2nd July, 1943

MS/1/Operating.

Mr. J. D. Stringer,
24 Westcott Street,
HULL.

Dear Sir,

We have received a report to the effect that once
again for the third time since the commencement of
hostilities, a vessel to which you were attached has
fallen a victim to enemy action, but it is gratifying
to know that as on previous occasions, you have reached
this country safely.

Although you have not apparently suffered any ill
effects following the loss of your last vessel, we feel
sure that the special leave of absence which has been
granted to you will be acceptable, and we sincerely hope
you will derive the fullest possible benefit from the
rest and change thus afforded.

Notwithstanding that the hopes we expressed after
your previous mishaps have not been realised, we tender
to you nevertheless our earnest good wishes for a safe
homecoming from all your future voyages.

Yours faithfully,
THE MARCONI INTERNATIONAL MARINE
COMMUNICATION COMPANY LIMITED

ASSISTANT GENERAL MANAGER (OPERATING AND TRAFFIC)

Your C.R.S.3. form is enclosed herewith.

'Letter from Marconi dated 2nd July 1943 following sinking of Holmbury' (Author's)

Chapter 8
SS Fort Capot River

When the Holmbury was hit and sunk in May 1943, Jack and the crew did not know that there was beginning to be a decisive change in the Battle of the Atlantic, in favour of the Allies. After the disastrous loss of Allied merchant ships two months earlier in March (one of the highest monthly losses in the war), a combination of economic, scientific and planning factors finally combined to turn the tide in the Allies' favour. The arrival of American long range Liberator aircraft helped close the mid-Atlantic air gap. Aircraft carriers were relocated from the Mediterranean to the Atlantic, to perform convoy duties. More R.A.F. aircraft were sent to the Bay of Biscay to attack German submarines. These measures had a devastating effect on the Axis U-Boat operations accounting for half of their losses and totalling 56 U-Boats destroyed in April and May. Improved radar and ASDIC (named after the Anti-Submarine Detection Investigation Committee) developments were being rapidly introduced by the Allies, together with superior anti-submarine weapons. The Allies assembled groups of destroyers and frigates, specifically to hunt for enemy submarines. Better integration of all these elements successfully disrupted the U-Boat wolfpacks. Alongside all this destruction there was a huge increase in production of American liberty merchant ships, up to 140 per month. The corresponding workforce had been increased from four thousand in 1941, to eighty thousand two years later. This meant that new ships were coming into service more quickly than ships were being destroyed. The consequence of all these actions resulted in the German command moving most of their submarines to areas closer to British coastal waters, away from the mid-Atlantic. Nevertheless, the U-boats that remained in the Atlantic, albeit fewer in number, remained a threat until the last day of the war.

Jack's next engagement, starting on the 17th of August, would now revolve around the new course the war was taking, in the fast-changing events of 1943. This would begin not far from his home, at the port of Immingham on the southwest bank of the River Humber, six miles from Grimsby. This was an important deepwater port which had been developed for coal exports just before the First World War. The port now also housed the Royal Navy Humber Force, consisting of flotillas of destroyers plus two cruisers, with oil storage facilities nearby. Alongside the jetty was the ship which would become Jack's home for the next seventeen months and it proved to be a pleasant surprise compared to his previous ships.

The Fort Capot River was a brand-new cargo carrying merchant ship which had only been completed on the 29th of May 1943. It was built in Canada to a design of the 'North Sands' type, so called because these ships conformed to the original British working drawings supplied by the North Sands shipyard of Thompson and Sons in Sunderland. The ships were designed with a deadweight of 9,300 tons, but all ships of this size were referred to as 10,000 tonners, as war time regulations allowed deeper loading. One ship with this capacity could provide enough provisions to feed a quarter of a million people per week during wartime. The Fort Capot River was constructed on Canada's West Coast in the North Vancouver Yard, which was the most prolific of Canada's shipyards. There were seven shipyards on the Canadian West Coast and eleven on the East Coast and Great Lakes combined. At the height of the war Canadian yards were producing one ship every three days. In total 374 ships were built, of similar design to each other. These ships were named either 'Fort' to be transferred to the British Government, or 'Park' to be used by the Canadian Government. They were the equivalent of the American Liberty vessels but were generally less well known.

The Fort Capot River had left Vancouver in early June loaded with lumber, phosphates and lead. The ship journeyed via the Panama Canal, Key West and New York. From New York the ship became part of a convoy heading to Loch Ewe in Scotland, before arriving in early August at Immingham, where she unloaded and awaited a new crew. The ship was under the experienced command of Captain Harold James Kay D.S.C. who had been awarded his honour following an attack on his previous vessel in May 1942. His ship had been travelling in convoy PQ.16 and was on its way to Murmansk in Russia, when it was struck by a bomb and damaged, but it still reached its destination, despite repeated attacks.

Jack was impressed with his new captain and delighted to see how much better his new vessel was compared to what he had previously experienced. He had a larger, more comfortable cabin, with hot and cold running water in the sink. The cabin was well fitted out with good lighting, a small desk and a chair, and a wardrobe. With two portholes, he could foresee that there would be more of a breeze when they were in hot and humid areas. Best of all, it was clean with no bugs! After leaving Immingham on the 17th of August, then picking up a cargo of coal from Tyneside, the vessel commenced its voyage around Britain with an overnight stop at Loch Ewe before steaming across the Atlantic heading for America.

Having had a trouble-free voyage across the Atlantic, stopping briefly at St. John's, Newfoundland, the Fort Capot River headed down to the largest estuary on the east coast of America, the two-hundred-mile-long Chesapeake Bay. With no radio watches to keep when they were in the safety of the bay, Jack relaxed, contemplated the peace of the autumnal scenery and admired the expansive sunset. The ship arrived at their destination of Baltimore on the 23rd of September.

After unloading their cargo, Jack and the crew went ashore at this major industrial centre where labourers were working day and night, to produce ships, planes and equipment for the war. Jack knew he had two weeks in Baltimore before they would depart again. Jack took this opportunity to buy himself some additional shoes and clothes as there were plenty here, in contrast to them being rationed in Britain. He experienced his first Chinese restaurant, and for the first time he noticed the segregation of black Americans in the back of the tramcars when travelling around the city. These black Americans had come from the southern states, to fill the vacancies in the booming factories.

Meeting up with other sailors at the Merchant Navy Club to compare conditions on each others' ships was always a favoured pastime. The sailors enjoyed the popular dances and weekly free cocktails, but the free beer nights had already been stopped due to overindulgence by some! Feelings of being in a constant state of danger and tension whilst at sea would often erupt when they were in port, as sailors were often desperate to unwind when they went ashore. On one occasion, when a queue was forming of sailors who were waiting for their wage allocation before going ashore, one of the firemen came storming in. He demanded to be given his money immediately. The second mate officer told him to wait, and the fireman shouted back,

"The sailors, it's always the fucking sailors. I want my money!"

The third engineer told him to leave the saloon, and the fireman retorted,

"Mind your own fucking business, you're only the third engineer!"

Before the situation got out of hand, with the possibility of a fight happening, the second mate told the fireman that no one would be paid until after he had left. The fireman departed and returned later at the correct time, having calmed down. He was fined a day's wages, which was ten shillings. One of the young galley boys went ashore without leave and he was brought back two days later by the military police, fined and reinstated. Finally, the cargo of ammunition and other military supplies, plus general cargo, were placed into the ship, and some trucks were loaded onto the deck. Two new crew were employed because two sailors had to go to hospital, one with stomach ulcers and another for treatment of scabies.

The Fort Capot River ship steamed back down the Chesapeake Bay into the wide channel at Hampton Roads, Virginia before entering the Atlantic Ocean. Jack saw that they were forming into the biggest convoy he had ever sailed in, comprising 85 merchant ships with an impressive convoy escort of 13 recently built American destroyers. Convoy UGS.20 (United States to Gibraltar, Slow), was the twentieth in a series of eastbound convoys from Hampton Roads. The first convoy had sailed in October 1942 to support the North African campaign. By the time that Jack's convoy set off on the 5th of October 1943, three convoys per month were heading towards the Mediterranean to support the Allied troops during the invasion of Italy, although it is likely that Jack and the crew did not know precisely where they would end up.

The voyage across the Atlantic was again trouble-free. The only distress signals that the radio operators heard were very faint although clear, but as they came from so far away, they did not indicate any immediate danger to their ship. Halfway across the ocean, the land station responsible for sending instructions via longwave to the Fort Capot River ship changed, from Washington D.C. (call sign NSS) to Rugby in England (call sign GBR). The radio officers had set times each hour for tuning their radio receivers to the specific longwave required to receive their next instructions for the ship. With no instructions being given during the rest of each hour, the radio officers reverted to listening on 500 kc/s (kilocycles per second) medium wave for any distress signals, but this was now mainly just atmospherics. This white noise could be very sleep inducing, particularly during the darkness of night, and Jack found that the mug of sweet tea brought to him by the steward halfway through his watch helped to keep him alert.

As the ship travelled nearer to Gibraltar, Jack heard the Spanish coastal stations working on the calling and distress frequency. This meant that his ship was now coming under the protection of the R.A.F. Coastal Command, and it was a relief to see them pass by or circle over the convoy from time to time. Accidents to seamen were always a risk and during this voyage two of the firemen were injured by falls of coal, and one sailor was swept along the deck whilst securing the scrambling nets and he crashed into some wooden supports. Thankfully none of them required hospital treatment. After eighteen days at sea the armada of ships passed through the Strait of Gibraltar and anchored just east of the Rock of Gibraltar. After the convoy re-formed the following day, Jack found that they were heading east through the Mediterranean. This was the first time he had been back to the Mediterranean since he was there just before the war on the cruise ship Arandora Star. Jack's convoy was now reduced to just seventeen other ships in addition to Jack's ship, with a British naval escort accompanying them. Most of the original convoy had diverted to Morocco or southern Italy, whereas Jack and the other crew on the Fort Capot River were now informed that their destination was to be Port Said in Egypt.

On the 1st of November the Fort Capot River lay at anchor in the warm sunshine, near to the entrance to the Suez Canal. The ship was awaiting smaller lighters to unload her cargo which would mainly be heading in other ships to India and the Far East. Warnings were given to all the crew not to venture into the city alone, especially if taking a water taxi at night, as there had been many reports of robberies and some cases of murder. Most of the crew did take the opportunity to explore the city, just to escape the heat on board during the day. Despite a few reported threats and extortionate demands for fares there were no serious incidents.

Not long after arriving in the port there was an argument with a local contractor who tried a common scam. When they were at sea, the ash and clinker were disposed of through a chute on the ship's side, which took place an hour after dark and when in convoy, to avoid leaving a floating trail. However, when they were in port the ash and clinker were stored on deck. The local contractor appeared, holding an allegedly official document, stating that he had a contract to remove the ash and clinker from the stokehold fires at the end of each watch. The Captain ordered him off the ship but after failing to leave he was lifted off his feet and deposited back in his boat. The constant stream of locals in their bum boats offered a whole range of wares including Arab trinkets, buckets of dates and fruits, Turkish Delight, and even dated sepia postcards of scantily dressed women from the 1920s. The crew in turn would then barter whatever was to hand such as their old worn-out clothes and their free weekly ration of the unpopular Victory V cigarettes. Even the cook was doing deals with the leftover scraps from their meals!

After almost two weeks, the ship was ordered to the main Egyptian port of Alexandria, just 150 miles to the west, where it arrived on the 17th of November. Here it quickly loaded its next cargo of assorted military materials under the direction of the local Transport Officer. The Transport Officers were usually experienced Merchant Navy officers, who had become Royal Navy reserves. There was a sense of urgency with loading taking place throughout the night, since following the Italians' surrender two months earlier the Allies were pushing forward against the Germans in the mainland of Italy. First to be loaded were large 40-gallon drums of high rated 100 octane fuel, which was used mainly for maximising the performance of aircraft engines to increase their top speed by about ten per cent. Next to be loaded were boxes of various calibres of ammunition which were stored in a separate secure hold with sawdust covering the steel floor. There followed an array of general stores to be loaded on board, in total amounting to over one thousand tons. Included were tents, clothing, blankets, medical equipment, corrugated steel for landing strips, generators, NAAFI (Navy, Army and Air Force Institutes) stores, tinned rations, canned beer and cigarettes. The bulk of the remainder of the holds, plus all the deck storage, was taken up with 120 motor transports, with only basic shelters being provided during the journey for the drivers of these vehicles.

Leaving Alexandria on the 23rd of November, Jack's ship joined a large convoy heading west to Gibraltar but on the second day they diverted north along with fourteen other vessels. After a voyage of 800 miles, they arrived at the southeast area of Sicily and anchored in the ten-mile bay, with the port of Augusta at the north, and the port of Syracuse to the south. It was here just four months earlier, that the SAS (Special Air Service) under Blair 'Paddy' Mayne had destroyed the

Italian coastal batteries with the ports quickly taken, in one of the first operations of the Allied Invasion of Sicily. By the time Jack's ship arrived here the Allies were advancing across the mainland and had occupied southern Italy, although they were meeting stiff German resistance. The following day, the 29th of November, the Fort Capot River left Sicily in convoy AH.10A. Nineteen ships sailed northeast into the Adriatic Sea, carrying between them a sizeable arsenal of supplies and motor transports to support the Allied army and air force on the mainland. Their final destination was 340 miles away, the port of Bari, just 150 miles south of the front line.

Midway through their voyage, through a message from the convoy commander, Jack became aware of a change of plan for some of the convoy. This decision would probably save his life and the lives of his fellow crew. The Fort Capot River and nine other vessels were ordered to go to the nearer port of Taranto, where they arrived on the 30th of November. The remaining nine vessels were told to continue onwards to Bari, where they arrived the following day, the 1st of December. This unexpected change of destination was made due to several unrelated circumstances.

Usually, there was a regular five-day cycle of ships arriving at Bari, to keep the number of ships to manageable levels. However, earlier in November there had been a period of bad weather in the Mediterranean and the Bay of Biscay. This meant that some ships were unable to travel to Bari on their original scheduled day. Consequently, there were far more ships and personnel all arriving at the same time. This was exacerbated by the lack of coordination between the military and naval authorities, resulting in too many convoys being rushed forward to Bari to keep up with the demands for supplies. The outcome of all this was that when the nine vessels who had left Jack's convoy arrived at Bari, a total of 38 ships were now crowded too closely together. Fourteen ships were moored stern-on to the perimeter seawall, almost touching one another. Further ships were also lying outside the harbour awaiting entrance. Other ships who had unloaded their cargo were anchored in the same area pending instructions to return in convoy to the south. The backlog of ships to be unloaded was further hampered by some ships that had arrived from North African and Middle Eastern ports, as they had been incorrectly loaded before departure. Bari was also short of dock gangs, as the workers who were being sent to Bari from a dock operating company in Naples, were delayed.

Unfortunately, on the 2nd of December, the packed harbour was noticed by Werner Hahn flying his Messerschmitt ME-210 reconnaissance plane high over the city, and he was able to make a second pass, uncontested, before heading home to his base to the north. The port was under the jurisdiction of the British because Bari was the main supply base for General Montgomery's Eighth Army. In addition, Bari had very recently been designated the headquarters of the American Fifteenth Airforce. Under the command of Major James 'Jimmy' Doolittle who had arrived just the day before, aircraft were gathering ready to bomb targets in the Balkans, Italy and Germany. Unfortunately, the failings in Bari's defences would become evident during that fateful night. The main telephone line between the Sector Operation Room and the anti-aircraft Gun Operation Room was out of action, as were most of the British radar systems in the area, which meant that warning times of any raids would be severely reduced. The R.A.F. dusk patrol had returned to base not long before the German raid commenced, and none of the R.A.F. Beaufort night fighters were in the air.

Believing the German Luftwaffe was no longer a threat this far south, British Air Vice Marshall Sir Arthur Conningham was confident that the Germans would never attack Bari.

Responding to questions at a press conference on that very afternoon of the 2nd of December, Conningham proclaimed,

"I would regard it a personal affront and insult if the Luftwaffe would attempt any significant action in this area."

Following sunset at around 4.30pm, the floodlights were switched on, so that the docks of Bari became bathed in light to allow the unloading to continue throughout the night, to ease the backlog. However, Field Marshall Wolfram von Richtofen (the cousin of the legendary pilot the Red Baron, of WW1 fame), having received the earlier reconnaissance reports, planned a raid on the docks immediately. A large force of 105 Junkers Ju-88 bombers took off from several bases in northern Italy, at first flying eastwards to the Adriatic. The bombers subsequently turned south, then flew west to further surprise the Allies, by attacking from that direction. They also dropped Duppel, thin strips of metal foil in varying lengths, to confuse radar systems. Although 17 of the bombers had to abort their mission before reaching the target, 88 planes did reach Bari on schedule.

It was a complete surprise when at 7.30pm the first bombers arrived over Bari dropping flares, but with the docks already brilliantly lit by the dock lights these were hardly needed. The first bombs missed the docks and fell on the city, causing panic to the local population, who until then had survived unscathed from any attacks during the war. However, the bombers quickly adjusted their aim, and the bombs fell rapidly on the docks and the ships moored there. One of the first to be hit was the American liberty ship Joseph Wheeler which had been in Jack's convoy AH.10A. This ship took a direct hit and exploded with the loss of all the 41 people on board. Working their way along the line of ships, one after another was hit. The chaos intensified further as a bulk gasoline pipeline on the shore was severed, causing fuel to leak out and spread before catching fire, engulfing other ships within the dock. Two smaller British tankers were hit, one of which sank, adding to the flammable content in the water. Crews worked frantically to free ships before they were overcome by flames, but many men were forced to jump into the harbour to try to escape the infernos.

After twenty minutes the last of the bombers departed, having lost only two planes. Just then, a massive explosion erupted into the night sky, as the John Harvey - another American liberty ship which was only completed at the beginning of the year - disappeared in a mushroom shaped fireball. Fire had spread quickly on the ship and it had ignited the cargo of ammunition it was carrying. Parts of the ship were hurled hundreds of feet into the air and all on board were killed instantly. The force of the explosion also knocked over people around the harbour.

What almost no one knew at the time was that this ship was also carrying a potentially deadly secret cargo, weighing about one hundred tons. This had comprised 2,000 liquid mustard gas bombs, each bomb looking essentially like a conventional bomb, being four feet long and eight inches in diameter. This poisonous gas shipment was shrouded in official secrecy and only a handful of people on board knew about the toxic nature of the cargo. The American government condemned the use of toxic gas but stated that they would reply in kind if the enemy used such a weapon first, so this shipment was to be held in reserve. One of the few people on board who had not been officially informed but became aware of the deadly substance of the cargo during their voyage from America, was Captain Knowles. Since the John Harvey had arrived at Bari four days previously, he had tried in vain to get the British port officials to speed up the discharging process. However, as he was bound to secrecy and the lethal gas was not officially on board, according to the port officials the unloading of the John Harvey did not warrant special priority.

There were several undamaged British motor torpedo boats stationed in the harbour for coastal force operations. These boats were used immediately to start rescuing the men trapped on burning ships and many others who were now in the thick oily water. Everyone was unaware about the liquid mustard gas that was now mixed in with the seawater, and more was still raining down from the sky even after several minutes. Men of several nationalities were pulled into rescue boats, including Norwegian, British, American, Italian, Polish, Dutch and Lascars. In the confusion, nobody seemed to notice the acrid fumes coming from the water. Many people went into the water to help to lift out those unable to climb aboard by themselves. Ships continued to catch fire and explode, and to drift from their moorings, with the rescue operation continuing unabated throughout the night.

The following morning there was a scene of utter devastation. Much of the old medieval part of the town was in ruins with parts still burning. Ships and areas around the harbour were also on fire, and a thick pall of black smoke hung over the city. Fortunately, there were several military and civilian hospitals in the area, but the staff were quickly overwhelmed by the hundreds of people requiring help. Everyone was oblivious of the mustard gas still on the survivors' clothes and bodies. This meant that many individuals were given just blankets to put over their wet clothes, and cups of tea, while they joined the long wait to be seen. It later transpired that these people who had been wrapped in blankets subsequently suffered worse burns and more of them died than people who were attended to immediately, due to the prolonged intensive exposure of the gas on their skin.

Gradually, other strange symptoms began to emerge amongst many of the patients. Many of the burnt patients began to have problems with their eyes, including pain, gross swelling and photophobia (a severe sensitivity to light). Skin lesions appeared, with some men developing enormous blisters and many having large patches of sore red skin. The distribution of these burns varied greatly and seemed to follow a pattern according to the amount of contact people had had with the water in the harbour. People who had been completely immersed in the harbour water were burnt all over, but those who had been only partly in the water were only burnt on the parts of their bodies that had been in the water. Some people had washed the thick oily slime from the harbour waters off their bodies and put on clean clothes, and these people were the least burnt, or even had no burns at all. Most worrying and perplexing were those patients who seemed to recover, only to die suddenly just a few minutes later for no apparent reason. Other symptoms occurred including respiratory problems, sore throats, nausea and vomiting, and a great thirst. Furthermore, some of the hospital staff became badly affected with blistering skin.

Doctors began to suspect that there had been some form of chemical attack from Germany, so urgent calls were made to the Allied Force Headquarters in Algeria for help. This resulted in Lieutenant Colonel Stewart Alexander, an expert in chemical warfare medicine, being dispatched to Bari on the 5th of December. Quickly and meticulously, he examined and spoke to many of the patients. He soon noticed a particular garlic-like smell, which he knew was associated with mustard gas. Numerous Italian civilians also started arriving, showing similar symptoms to the naval and military personnel, as they too had been affected by the cloud of poisonous gas blowing over the city.

Over the next few days, despite being told repeatedly that no chemical bombs had been on any Allied ships, Lieutenant Colonel Alexander was not convinced. Therefore, he carefully considered all the information he had been given and everything that he had learnt from the people's injuries and symptoms. He studied a map showing the location of all the ships before the raid had started. He noted the varied locations of the survivors and how that related to the severity of their injuries. He organised a variety of tests to be done on the surviving patients and requested that comprehensive autopsies were to be performed on patients who had died unexpectedly. He had the thick oily harbour water analysed. The result of all his analysis on the range of data collected, led him to the source of the mustard gas being in the area around the John Harvey ship. A diver even recovered a bomb casing from the depths of the water, which was identified as being an American mustard shell. Officials denied that there had been mustard gas on board the John Harvey, but Lieutenant Alexander had worked it out.

There were around one thousand marine and military casualties, and possibly at least a similar number of civilians, but the full extent would never be known as many of the civilians had fled the city after the raid. A total of 26 Allied and Italian ships of all sizes had been sunk. These were mostly cargo ships, three of which were later salvaged. Fourteen other ships suffered varied degrees of damage and there had been a huge loss of valuable cargoes. Apart from Pearl Harbour, this was the worst single shipping disaster during the war. The port was out of action completely for over a week and did not fully reopen for two months. The Allied push against the Germans further north was limited because of this attack, and there was a significant reduction in operations for the American 15th Airforce over the following three months.

The detailed report that Lieutenant Colonel Alexander wrote on the 27th of December regarding the Bari attack and the injuries caused by the mustard gas, was immediately classified by the Allied commanders so that Hitler could not use it as an excuse to launch a gas attack. Any mention of mustard gas was removed from all medical records, with causes of injuries and death replaced with 'due to enemy action'. The Allies did not know that the Germans had already suspected that the Allies were stockpiling gas supplies in Italy. After the air raid, an Italian frogman sympathetic to the Germans' cause recovered part of a M47 bomb casing, confirming the Germans' suspicions. The Bari attack and all mention of gas remained hidden from the public for many years after the war ended. Remarkably there was one positive from the raid. Alexander had noted the effects of the gas on the white blood cells of casualties. He later used this discovery to conduct further experiments, which would eventually lead to the development of chemotherapy treatments against cancer.

Back in Taranto, Jack and the crew were still at anchorage when the attack on Bari occurred. The unloading situation here was slow, as there was limited capacity for unloading stores, due to there being only two alongside berths needed to allow for direct loading or unloading. There was also restricted rail clearance and there were inadequate warehouse depots. A delayed convoy of twelve ships, which had arrived three days before them, was only a quarter of the way through unloading. News of the air raid on Bari meant everyone was on high alert as Taranto was only 50 miles south of them overland and less than 15 minutes of flying time away. Fortunately, no further air raids were carried out, possibly partly due to the deteriorating winter weather with several days of thunderstorms, patches of fog and cloudy skies. Jack and the crew on board the Fort Capot River noticed the arrival of two damaged British destroyers from Bari two days after the attack. H.M.S. Bicester was being towed into port by H.M.S. Zetland. What Jack could not have known was that additional help had to be provided by dock pilots and merchant officers from Taranto, to enable these ships to safely anchor. By the time they arrived in Taranto the navigating officers on board the two destroyers were all having difficulties with their vision, as a consequence of the gas explosion at Bari. It took two weeks before the Fort Capot River was unloaded and ready to leave Taranto, in convoy, to sail back south to Augusta, Sicily. The crew on the Fort Capot River were counting their blessings, because as they had been diverted to Taranto, they had been lucky to escape the attack at Bari. Of the nine ships from their convoy that had continued to Bari, three had been sunk, three were badly damaged, and three survived with minor damage.

At the end of December 1943, Jack returned to Alexandria in Egypt. During 1944 this route soon became familiar to Jack. He made three more return trips on the Fort Capot River, sailing from Alexandria to Sicily to Taranto, with a round trip of over two thousand miles each time. The cargoes remained the same. On each trip the ship was loaded with general stores, ammunition and around a hundred or more motor transport vehicles, to feed the Allies' grinding progression northwards through the Italian mainland. Following the surrender of Italy in September 1943, the only enemy submarines now operating in the Mediterranean were decreasing numbers of German U-Boats. These were based mainly in Toulon, although there were additional small bases in Pola (now Pula in Croatia) in the far northeast of the Adriatic Sea, and in Salamis close to Athens in Greece. These totalled fewer than 20 U-Boats at the beginning of 1944 with on average only five on patrol at any one time. The total number of Allied ships sunk in 1944 totalled only 21, compared to 86 in 1943.

During the time that Jack was making these voyages, one merchant ship was sunk near Italy, eight were sunk off the western coast of North Africa, and one ship was destroyed in the eastern Mediterranean Sea near Cyprus. This was the least hazardous period Jack had experienced personally during the war. In February 1944, The Fort Capot River was sent to the Port of Bari which was trying to fully reopen to shipping. The ship's propeller hit an obstacle under the water when it was being manoeuvred alongside the wharf. After towing the stern clear, a sunken craft floated to the surface. Clearly, reopening the port was proving to be a long operation.

To the crew's surprise, in May 1944 the Fort Capot River was ordered to go in the opposite direction from Port Said. Carrying a cargo of coal, they steamed through the Suez Canal, heading for the Port of Durban in South Africa. During their journey, the last Allied vessel was sunk in the Mediterranean. This was the Fort Missanabie, which was a British ship, of a type similar to the Fort Capot River. The ship was sunk on the 19th of May between Taranto and Sicily, on the exact route Jack and his crew had been travelling for the last five months. Being sent on a different route this time had proved to be their good fortune.

This alternative voyage to South Africa turned out to be a welcome relief for the crew and gave them an extended break from the activities of war. All U-Boats had been withdrawn from the South African coast since August 1943 due to difficulties in re-supplying them, following complete air and naval dominance by the Allies. Their stay was further extended as repairs to the ship were needed. Durban was a city thronging with Allied military personnel, many on their way to Europe or Burma. Jack was surprised by the nightly blackouts which had been enforced over the city, and for as far as ten miles inland. The blackouts had begun after a single Japanese plane was spotted over the city two years previously, in order to make sure that visiting warships were not illuminated by the shore lights. Celebrating the news of the D-Day landings, Jack and the crew felt they were due some respite after almost five years of constant danger.

They took advantage of the warm weather and wide sandy beaches, and enjoyed being in such a modern clean city with good food. On trips further afield, they experienced the wide, open grasslands of the veldt and saw large groups of zebras, deer and giraffes.

In Durban there was a middle-aged South African woman, Perla Gibson, nicknamed 'The Woman in White,' who was a former soprano singer. Beginning in April 1940, she would stand on the North Pier by the narrow harbour entrance or on the quayside and, using a megaphone, she sang popular songs to all the troopships, convoys and hospital ships entering or leaving the harbour. This became an unforgettable experience witnessed regularly by the ship's crew. Throughout the war she never missed one convoy, whatever the weather, even performing on the day when she received the news that her oldest son had been killed in action. It was estimated that she sang to over 5,000 ships and around a quarter of a million troops. Perla's repertoire covered all the main British popular songs, and she sang South African folk songs for the South African troops. She sang arias from Wagner and Verdi for the Poles, Czechs and Greeks, the 'Star-Spangled Banner' for the Americans, 'Waltzing Matilda' for the Australians, and the 'Red, White and Navy Blue' for the New Zealanders. With troops and crews joining in and shouting for other requests, she once sang for six hours non-stop to some British 'Tommies' whom she adored. Jack and the crew sang back to her as they left, loaded with various food stocks, in a small convoy of six ships heading back northwards, in July 1944.

The scorching summer heat passing through the Red Sea and the Suez Canal was particularly bad for the firemen and trimmers working in the inferno of the stokehold. These men needed to use rags just for going down the ladder, to avoid burning their hands, and they took extreme care not to touch a bulkhead, as it was so hot it could scorch their body on contact. When their vessel was required to wait at the large saltwater Great Bitter Lake on the canal, to allow warships and tankers priority of passage, relief finally came as many of the crew took advantage of the delay to enjoy a cooling swim in the warm crystal-clear salt waters.

Arriving back in Alexandria, Egypt in early August, Jack reverted to the military convoy supply routes to Italy for most of the rest of the year. In Italy, the fighting was raging on, involving one million men on both sides, with the Allies' advance being painfully slow. The good news was that the last operational U-Boat in the Mediterranean was destroyed in heavy bombing of the Germans' base at Toulon, France, which was quickly followed by the Allies successfully invading Southern France over the next month. After replacing two injured sailors and four other crew who tested positive for venereal disease, Jack's ship continued shuttling the supply of military vehicles to Brindisi and Bari. Then they travelled more than 200 miles further north up the east coast, to deliver more military supplies to Ancona. Now they were only 50 miles from the frontline, in a city that had just been captured by Polish forces ten weeks previously.

During their stay at Brindisi, one incident occurred on board the ship which Jack thought was particularly shocking. One afternoon, they were all waiting for their orders to sail, when suddenly the officers heard some of the crew shouting up to them for help. Rushing down from their mess room, Jack and the first mate and second mate reached the aft quarters of the firemen, to find one of them sitting on the floor, with a deep stab wound in the centre of his back which was pouring with blood. Standing near to the injured fireman was one of the sailors, swearing and drunk, and holding a fire axe which was covered with blood. The three officers jumped on the sailor, took the fire axe from him and marched him to a storeroom, where he was locked in and handcuffed by the Captain. While Jack used his first aid skills to try to quell the fireman's bleeding, the first mate got the jolly boat to the shore to bring a doctor from the naval house back to the ship. The military police soon removed the drunk sailor and took him ashore to the guard house, whilst the injured fireman went to hospital for treatment. Neither of them returned to the ship before it left. Quarrels and drunkenness were not uncommon, especially during shore leave, but this was the worst incident witnessed by Jack during his time at sea.

After completing another round trip to Ancona, the Fort Capot River was ordered to Naples on the west coast of Italy. On the 21st of November they arrived at Naples, a city that Jack had never been to before. Naples had been captured by the Allies a year earlier but it had already been heavily damaged, first by large air strikes from the Allies and then by the scorched earth policy by the Germans prior to their departure. This had left the city with no clean drinking water and no sewage system, causing a prevailing foul smell throughout the destroyed streets, hence it became known to Allied service men as 'the armpit of the Mediterranean.' In addition, there was a severe shortage of food, transport and electricity, leading to people starving and the city being in chaos and overrun with crime. Furthermore, the population had expanded significantly eight months previously, as about twelve thousand people had fled to Naples from surrounding villages, following the eruption of Mount Vesuvius on the 17th of March 1944, only seven miles from the outskirts of the city. This was the worst eruption for 72 years, spewing rocks, lava and ash to the surrounding area, and even destroying 88 American planes at the nearby Pompeii Airfield. Jack and two of his colleagues paid a taxi driver to take them on a rare trip away from the docks, to see the fields blackened by ash from the volcano, and the villages damaged by the lava. They then enjoyed a meal and some wine at a local restaurant which was owned by the taxi driver's family, and they kindly left a generous tip to show their appreciation.

The crew were glad to leave the city on the 11th of December, after a three week stay, hoping they were heading home for Christmas. However, their destination turned out to be West Africa, and they arrived at Freetown, Sierra Leone on Christmas Day, before heading to Takoradi, Ghana to load their last cargo of bauxite. Leaving Takoradi on the 9th of January 1945, they sailed independently around the west of Africa to join other ships from Casablanca. The following day they merged with convoy MKS.79G which had departed Gibraltar and totalled 28 vessels, plus four escorts and was destined for Britain. These cargo vessels were loaded mostly with raw materials for industry, including iron ore and phosphates. There were also four ships full of boxes of oranges, which had been in such short supply in Britain during most of the war but were now finally becoming more readily available to be transported to Britain.

During their return voyage, Jack had only picked up distress calls from one ship, which was on the other side of the Atlantic, near Canada. Worryingly, as they continued their voyage and got closer to home, four more ships around the British shores were torpedoed. Most of the declining numbers of submarines were now operating around British waters. To counteract this threat, additional escorts accompanied their convoy over the final two days. Now with eight escorts, the Fort Capot River continued without incident and reached its final port of call, Newport in South Wales on the 1st of February 1945. Three days later, after almost eighteen months away, Jack left the ship for his final time, as the war was almost reaching its dramatic conclusion.

'The Fort Capot River, name changed after the war' (The Allen Collection)

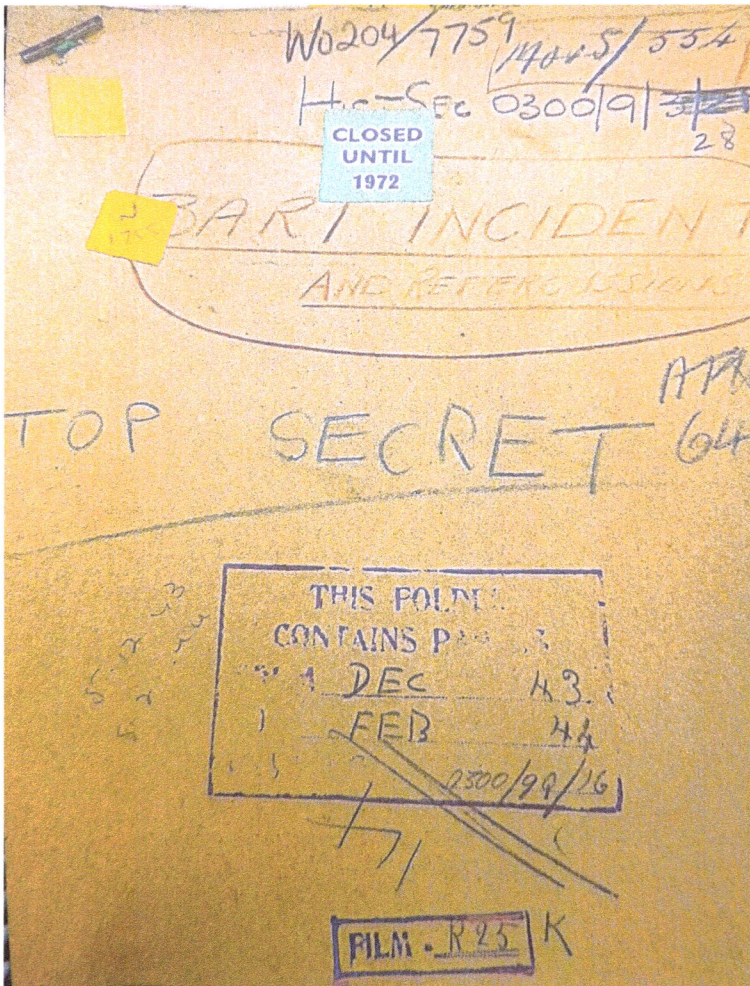

'File regarding Bari Air Raid,
2nd December 1943' (Kew National
Archives)

'Bari Harbour, ships still burning the day after the air raid' (Alamy, colour by Grant Kemp)

'Bari Harbour, 3rd December 1943' (WW2 Museum, New Orleans, colour Grant Kemp)

Chapter 9
SS City of Exeter and SS Fort Connolly

Jack had been very much looking forward to his six weeks of leave. He and his family were desperately hoping for the war to end before he would have to return to sea. Given that Jack had survived thus far, the thought that he might yet be attacked in the final weeks was uppermost in all their minds. What they did not yet know, was that the danger during these final months was to come from the last desperate and pointless air attacks by the Luftwaffe on Hull.

In the early hours of Christmas Eve, just six weeks before Jack arrived back in Hull, the Germans had launched a V1 rocket attack on the North of England, using modified Heinkel bombers, for terror and propaganda purposes. Although German aircraft released 45 flying bombs from over the sea just east of the Lincolnshire coastline, with the aim of hitting Manchester directly west, just 31 managed to cross over the shoreline and only 15 reached the Manchester surrounds, killing 42 civilians. The remaining rockets went astray, with four flying north. One ended up in the River Humber and three others exploded to the northwest of Hull resulting in some damage to a row of houses but no casualties.

Two further futile air raids occurred during Jack's time of leave in Hull. In the early hours of Sunday the 4th of March, the sirens went off. This was quickly followed by anti-aircraft fire, as a few German aircraft swooped low down above the city and haphazardly fired their cannon shells, hitting houses, cars, shops and roads. One of the planes made a pass along Ings Road, just over half a mile away from Jack's family's home. Incredibly, no one was hit, although there were numerous near misses and some small house fires.

Almost two weeks later, another air raid proved to be more serious and was another close call for Jack. During the early spring evening of Saturday the 17th of March, Jack was with his father and some of their neighbours in their busy local pub, the Crown Inn, on Holderness Road. They were discussing the latest war news, as the Germans had been pushed back over the Rhine River and in desperation were calling up boys as young as 15 or 16 years to fight. A substantial number of civilians were still out and about in the dark streets of East Hull that night as many were returning home from the city centre, feeling confident that they would be safe at this stage of the war. Even when the air raid sirens started at around 9.30pm, people were not particularly concerned, believing it was just another false alarm. Shortly afterwards, a lone Heinkel bomber roared over the city and swooping down on Holderness Road it dropped several fragmentation bombs less than half a mile from the Crown Inn. Jack and the other customers in the pub froze, expecting further explosions, but thankfully none came. Within minutes people from outside soon rushed into the bar and shouted that there were casualties in the road. Hearing the bells from the emergency services, several patrons including Jack ran outside to see if they could help.

Several more people came out of their houses to help. Buses had stopped on the road near the scene of the explosions and the passengers were running away, looking for shelter and comfort. By the time Jack arrived near the scene, he could see several bodies lying in the street near the Savoy Cinema, while some of the injured were being attended to by emergency workers and the public. Several side roads had been bombed, and ambulances were now trying to get closer to the area but were hindered by the many cars which had been abandoned. Jack and some of the other customers from the pub pushed these cars onto the pavements, to clear a path for the ambulances.

In all 12 people died at the scene of the bombing, and one person died a few days later, with another 22 needing to be hospitalised. Among the dead was a 71-year-old retired docker who had run from his house to shield a boy from the shrapnel, but tragically they both died. Sadly, among the dead was the mother of one-month-old twins, and a soldier home on leave. This turned out to be the last piloted raid of the war from an enemy aircraft on Britain. The final V1 and V2 rocket attacks occurred less than two weeks later in the London area.

The day after the air raid, Jack received news that he would be required on another ship in a few days' time. Before then, he was delighted to meet up with his cousin whom he had not seen since early in the war. His name was also Jack Stringer, and he had recently returned from America, having trained as a pilot to serve with Coastal Command. Jack's remaining days of leave were spent meeting up with family, often travelling on the back of his cousin's Panther motorbike.

Jack's final ship during the war was the old cargo and passenger steamship SS City of Exeter of 9,500 tons. This ship built in 1914 was owned by the Ellerman Lines Ltd and was used extensively during the First World War as a troopship. She had led a charmed life during the Second World War, safely completing numerous trips from the UK to India and Africa, picking up cargoes and carrying up to two hundred passengers at a time. By the time Jack reported on board the City of Exeter at Hull docks on the 21st of March 1945, he assumed that he would be travelling on this same route. A week later, the ship left Hull and joined a series of short convoys travelling around Britain, with their destination being the Clyde in Scotland. Sailing via Gravesend, this was going to be the first time Jack had sailed along the English Channel and around the south coast of England since the start of the war. Although the German U-Boat fleet was being decimated, particularly with heavy bombing raids on their ports, a small number were still active around the British Isles, as Jack would soon hear in the radio room.

Passing the Kent coast on the morning of the 6th of April, he heard a nearby distress call just off the coast of the Isle of Wright. This alerted him to a submarine attack on the SS Cuba, a large Vichy French passenger ship that had been captured by the British in 1940 and converted to a troopship capable of carrying over 1,200 passengers. The SS Cuba was sailing from Le Harve, France, across the channel to Southampton, with just 42 military personnel and her crew of 223. Fortunately, the ship was not travelling in the opposite direction, as it would have been packed with troops. Luckily, all but one of those on board were quickly rescued by her escorts. The submarine involved, U-1195, was tracked down and sunk shortly afterwards by a British destroyer, off Spithead Roads close to the Isle of Wight.

The City of Exeter was diverted further south in the Channel due to the nearby attack and reached Milford Haven in South Wales on the 8th of April, before setting off again, almost immediately, for the River Clyde in Glasgow. The crew were on high alert because another U-Boat had been in action on their intended route off the coast of North Wales. This U-Boat had sunk the American Liberty ship, the James Nesmith on the 7th of April. When the City of Exeter reached the Clyde on the 10th of April, Jack was glad that they would be waiting there for more than two weeks whilst there was a change of some of the crew. Military supplies were loaded and personnel boarded, and Jack and the crew waited to find out where they were to be sent to next.

It was becoming obvious that the war was probably only days away from an Allied victory, as the Allies were closing in on Berlin. Although, for the Merchant Navy, the threat of attack would be present until the very end. The City of Exeter left the Clyde and joined Convoy OS.125 which had come from Liverpool and now comprised 29 vessels and 11 escorts. Jack soon heard another nearby distress message coming from a ship which was being attacked by a German submarine. This time, the British destroyer, H.M.S. Redhill, was being torpedoed off the North Welsh coast. At the same time, German midget submarines were also in action off the East Coast of England. After a few days, tensions gradually receded as the convoy continued to head south, moving further away from British waters, and from the few remaining active German submarines. As they sailed around the northwest coast of Spain and the convoy dispersed, on the 1st of May they received the tumultuous news that Hitler was dead, having killed himself the previous day.

Over the next few days, the whole crew eagerly awaited the broadcasts being received in the radio room, as each day dramatic news unfolded. There was the fall of Berlin, and the recapture of Rangoon in Burma, the surrender of German troops in Italy, and the death or capture of leading Nazi officials. As the ship passed Gibraltar on the 5th of May, Jack heard of the liberation of Holland. Finally, the message everyone had been waiting for came through on the afternoon of Tuesday the 8th of May. This was in another Marconigram message, which came from the Admiralty and was marked 'Immediate.'

'Germany has surrendered unconditionally stop

Ceasefire has been ordered from 2201 GMT eighth May stop

Pending further orders all existing instructions regarding the defence security and control of Merchant Shipping are to remain in force stop

Merchant ships at sea whether in convoy or sailing independently are to continue their voyages as previously ordered.'

After almost two thousand days of war, the battle for Europe was finally over. Jack celebrated in the evening, by enjoying a drink with the Captain and other officers in the mess room. The warm glow from the sunset lit up the Atlas Mountains, as they steamed east along the North African coast. Up until the very last hours, shipping was being attacked by German submarines. The last victims were the Canadian cargo ship Avondale Park and the Norwegian cargo ship Sneland 1. They were hit within minutes of each other just after 11pm on the 7th of May 1945, near the Isle of May in the Firth of Forth, Scotland, with a loss of nine men.

For Jack, this voyage was his last in a convoy. The City of Exeter proceeded independently, first to Port Said, then through the Suez Canal and on to its destination of Bombay (now Mumbai) in India. Reaching India at the end of May, the ship carried supplies, mail and personnel around the coast, including to Ceylon (now Sri Lanka), before heading back to Britain with a cargo of cotton, arriving in Liverpool on the 12th of August 1945. Having missed out on the celebrations of the ending of war in Europe three months earlier, at last Jack was able to be home to enjoy the news of the surrender of Japan on the 15th of August. It was his 25th birthday a few days later. Having spent almost 900 days at sea, excluding time in port, and travelled over 200,000 miles throughout the war, he knew how lucky he had been to survive unscathed. As he and his friend Sam Burwell had now both ended their war-time experiences, they celebrated together and continued to remain in contact throughout their lives.

Following the ending of the war Jack decided to make one final trip with the Merchant Navy. He wanted to enjoy the experience of peacetime travel again, and he hoped to save some money, ready to start a new life and begin a new career. He boarded his last ship in Manchester, on the 21st of September. This was another modern Canadian Fort cargo vessel, the Fort Connolly and other than the British officers, the rest of the crew consisted of forty Chinese sailors. This voyage of 15 months took him around the world. He saw for himself the rapidly changing world, as countries moved from colonial rule to independent states.

Following the transport of general cargoes to Canada, the Fort Connolly headed back east. The ship conveyed goods and passengers around the coast of India, finally arriving on Christmas Eve in Madras (now Chennai) for repairs. After four weeks, in January 1946 the ship was ready to depart. The crew were given instructions to head to the Far East for motor transport duties. This proved to be fortuitous, as they were out of the area when the Indian Navy Mutiny occurred on 18th February. This affected all ports, beginning with protests against poor general working conditions, which then developed into widespread rioting and increasing demands for independence.

Now in the Far East, Jack's next port of call at the end of January was more than two thousand miles southeast to the Indonesian island of Java, and the port of Soerabaya (now Surabaya), the county's second largest city. Having been a Dutch colony, it had been captured by the Japanese in March 1942 but was bypassed by the Americans towards the end of the war. The local nationalists then started to take control before the British Indian Army arrived on behalf of the Dutch in October 1945, which resulted in a major battle the following month, with several thousand people dying. When Jack arrived two months later tensions were still high, security was strict, and he was surprised to see there was an abundance of unarmed Japanese soldiers still present, with many working in the docks. British forces left toward the end of the year and the Dutch agreed to full independence two years later.

The remainder of Jack's time over the next five months in the Far East included trips to Singapore, the Philippines and Japan, moving large amounts of military transports. Next, his ship headed to the Pacific Coast of America, then through the Panama Canal to Norfolk, Virginia, on the East Coast. Finally, he arrived back at his home port of Hull on the 28th of December 1946. He had completed his time at sea, having been away for fifteen months, and now aged 26 years old he had seen the world.

Jack left Marconi's employment on the 14th of February 1947, following the end of his leave period. Not long afterwards, he moved to London to begin his new life working for Shell Tankers in their new offices on the South Bank at Waterloo. He continued to work for Shell Tankers for 30 years and kept up his interest in Morse code throughout his life. He even spent several years as a Royal Navy Reservist, during the 1960s, working one or two evenings a week at N.A.T.O.'s Maritime Command headquarters in Northolt, monitoring Russian submarines. It was a big change being the hunter, rather than the hunted.

'Jack on the right, with his cousin also called Jack, March 1945'
(Author's, colour by Grant Kemp)

'The Crown Pub, Holderness Road, Hull, V.E. Day, 8th May 1945'
(Nicky Guest-Walmsley, colour by Grant Kemp)

'SS City of Exeter' (Alamy)

'SS Fort Connolly' (The Allen Collection)

'Soerabaya port, Java, Indonesia, January 1946, with graffiti reading we don't want foreign intervention.' (Author's, colour Grant Kemp)

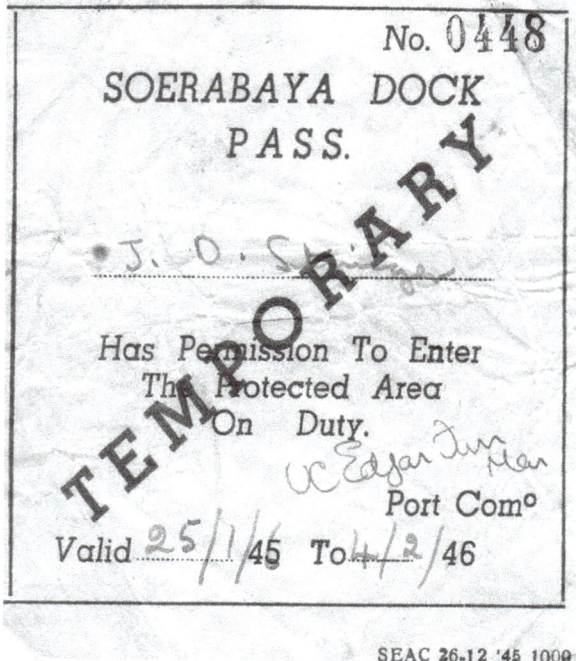

'Soerabaya Dock pass'
(Author's)

'Japanese invasion money'
(Author's)

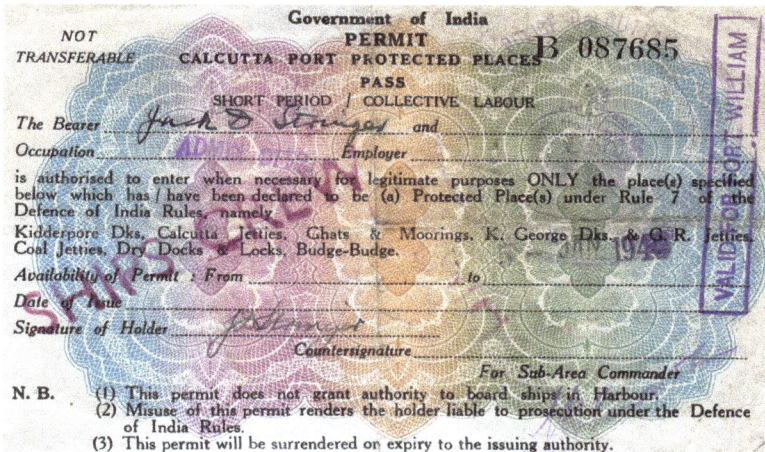

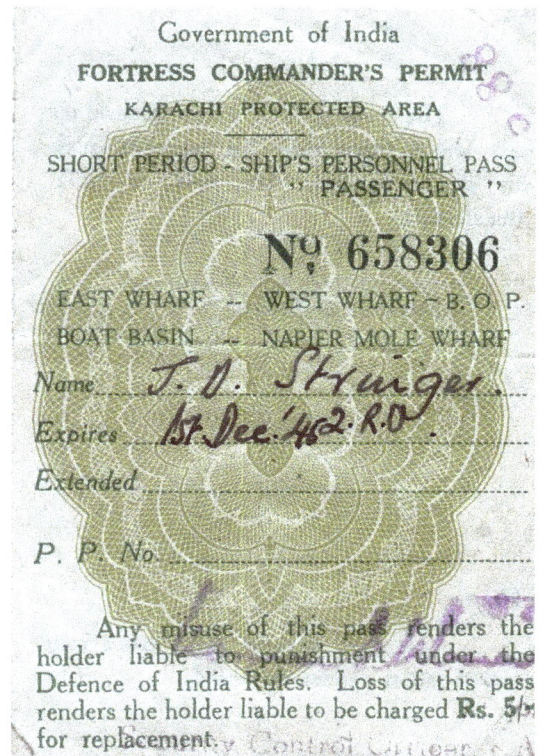

'Three photos of Jack's various dock passes'

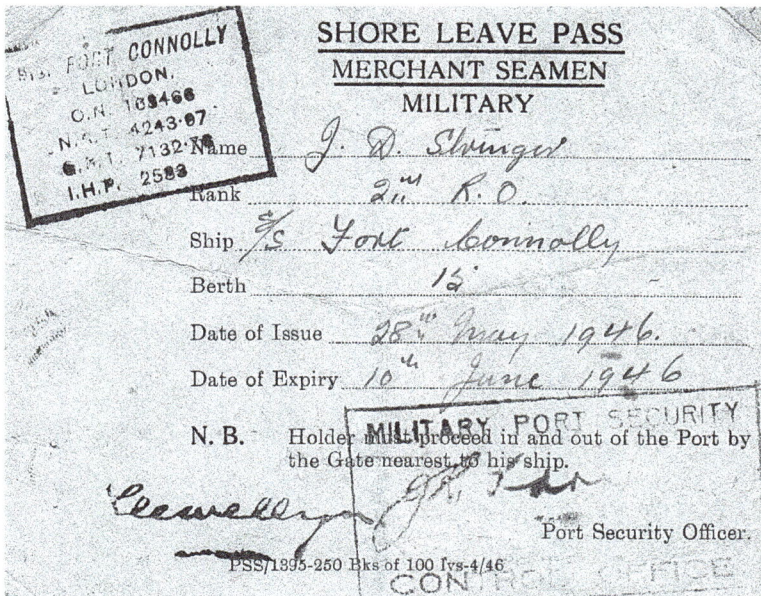

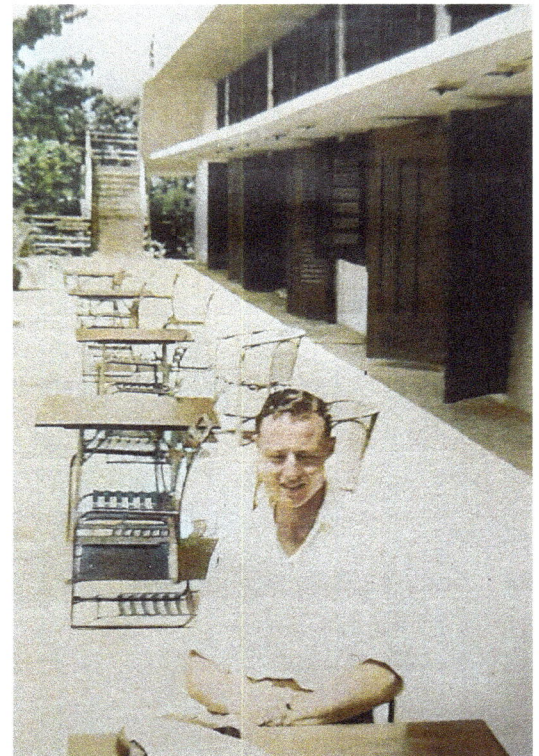

'Jack relaxing in Singapore,
May 1946'
(Author's photos)

'Jack's war service medals
From the left: The 1939-1945 Star, The Atlantic Star, The Africa Star,
The Italy Star, The War Medal' (Author's)

'Jack by the NATO refuelling depot at Loch Ewe, Scotland, 1998,
ashore here for the first time' (Author's)

The Wider Context

Around 185,000 men served in the Merchant Navy during the Second World War. More than 35,000 were lost at sea, although the true number will probably never be known. Nearly 24,000 names are listed on the memorial at Tower Hill, London, commemorating those who died at sea and have no other grave.

Numbers of Radio Officers lost reflected those in the rest of the Merchant Navy. At least 1,406 Radio Officers from all companies in the Merchant Navy lost their lives, of which 980 were from the Marconi Company, who had over 9,000 personnel at sea. A further 585 Marconi staff were disabled because of enemy action.

Over 500 boys aged 16 years or younger were killed whilst serving in the Merchant Navy, of which at least fifteen were only 14 years old. The oldest casualty was 79 years of age.

In addition, an HMSO (Her Majesty's Stationery Office) study published in 1955, 'Merchant Shipping and the Demands of War', states that between 1942-1944 as many as 11,600 Merchant Seamen either died shortly after leaving their ship, or their lives were permanently damaged, whether physically or mentally. Figures before and after that period were never calculated.

Around 4,500 British Merchant Seamen were taken illegally as prisoners of war by the Germans and held in Milag Nord P.O.W. Camp near Bremen, with more than a further 2,000 taken and held elsewhere.

There was scant support for the injured, or families of the dead. One in seven merchant sailors were killed during this war, which was a higher proportion of military personnel killed than in the three fighting services. Despite this, there was little recognition of the crucial role they played in the war.

Finally, for those Merchant Seamen not needed at the end of hostilities they were required to carry out two years of National Service, often in the Army, if they had not served five years during the war.

The Merchant Navy, the forgotten Fourth Service.

(Adapted from author Billy McGee and from Marconi records)

Fates of the submarines, and their commanders, that torpedoed Jack's ships

U-Boat 37 (sunk SS Heminge, September 1940)

Built in August 1938, in Bremen, Germany, U-37 was a type 1X long range ocean going U-Boat of 1,400 tons with a crew of 48-56 men, having eleven separate commanders during the war. U-37 was the sixth most successful U-Boat in terms of merchant tonnage sunk - 200,124 tons, being 53 merchant vessels. This U-Boat also sunk two warships and damaging one other merchant vessel, giving a total tonnage of 212,022. All these attacks were carried out during 11 war patrols from September 1939 to March 1941, totalling 280 days at sea. The first six patrols commenced from Wilhelmshaven, Germany. From August 1940, she was based in Lorient, France, from where she sunk Jack and the Heminge in September 1940. During this active time, she was attacked twice by an aircraft and surface ships but suffered only minor damage.

For the rest of the war U-37 was attached to training flotillas in the Baltic Sea, leaving the last one, Stettin, when it was captured by the Russians on the 26th of April 1945, arriving off Fensburg, Denmark, where it was scuttled at the end of the war on the 8th of May 1945. Unlike many other U-Boats, U-37 did not suffer any casualties.

Commander Victor Oehrn

Born on the 21st of October 1907 at Kedabeg, Russia, Victor Oehrn began his naval career in 1927, firstly on light cruises. Then in July 1935 he was one of the first officers to transfer to the newly commissioned U-Boat service. He became commander of U-14 in January 1936, taking it into Spanish waters during the civil war from July to September 1936.

At the outbreak of WW2, he joined the naval staff of Admiral Donitz. On the 15th of May 1940 he began his active patrol period on U-37, which lasted until the 22nd of October 1940. He spent a total of 81 days at sea, sinking 24 ships (104,846 tons) and damaging one (9,494 tons), making him the twenty-eighth most successful U-Boat ace, earning the Iron Cross and Knights Cross at that time.

He was brought back to the naval staff, taking command of the Mediterranean U-Boats, but during a mission in North Africa in July 1942 he was severely wounded and captured. He was released in an exchange of prisoners in October 1943, spending the rest of the war in several staff positions. He died in 1997 aged 90.

Italian Submarine Luigi Torelli (Sunk SS Urla, January 1941)

This virtually unique submarine was one of only two ships to serve in all three of the Axis navies. Completed in January 1940 in La Spezia, Italy, she was one of six Marconi class ocean-going submarines of 1,400 tons and a crew of 57.

After completion of training the Torelli left the Mediterranean as part of the first group of submarines at the newly established Atlantic base of Bordeaux, arriving on the 5th of October 1940. From this time until the end of 1941 the Torelli was operating in the North Atlantic. This submarine sank five merchant vessels totalling 26,500 tons, including Jack and the Urla in January 1941, and helped in the rescue of 254 German sailors from the German raider Atlantis that December. In early 1942 the Torelli began operations along the American coast sinking two merchants totalling 16,500 tons, but after surviving two serious air attacks which killed two crew, she was to perform a new role.

She was one of seven Italian submarines adapted to transport duties to the Far East in June 1943, to acquire precious and rare materials, including secretly taking a Japanese officer and German engineers to Japan, under German command. Shortly after arriving, the Italian armistice occurred, so the Torelli operated with both German and Italian crew and was renamed UIT-25. With the German supply tanker ships in the Indian Ocean destroyed in 1944 she had no choice but to remain in the Far East, ferrying goods between S.E. Asia and Japan, until the German surrender in May 1945. She was then taken over by the Japanese and renamed, yet again, to I-504, retaining some of the Italian crew until the 30th of August 1945 and the Japanese surrender. She finally met her end when she was scuttled by the American Navy in April 1946, at Kobe, Japan.

Commander Primo Longobardo

Born on the 19th of October 1901 in La Maddalena, Sardinia, Longobardo joined the naval academy at just 14 years old. He rose quickly through the ranks, seeing service in China from 1929-1932, then commanded several submarines, including during Italy's involvement in the Spanish Civil War in 1937, gaining a silver medal. In 1940 he was based at Pula Adriatic Naval Base, but he soon demanded action. He took command of the Torelli during January 1941, sinking four merchant vessels totalling 17,500 tons, the Urla being the last one.

Another shore period followed at Pula until in 1942 he took command of one of his previous submarines, the Calvi. On the evening of the 14th of July 1942, they were ordered to attack Convoy SL.115 comprising 29 merchants and four escorts, off the Azores, en route from Freetown to Liverpool, but they were spotted and depth charged by HMS Lulworth. Forced to come to the surface, Longobardo tried to outrun the escort and fired two torpedoes at it, which missed. The Calvi was raked by machine gun fire, which killed Longobardo and several crew before the submarine was abandoned and later capsized. When he was killed, Primo Longobardo was aged 41.

U-Boat 123 (sunk the SS Holmbury, May 1943)

Built 1939/1940 in Bremen, Germany, U-123 was a Type 1XB long-range ocean-going submarine of 1,430 tons total and a crew of 48-56 men.

This famous submarine had a long and distinguished history, carrying out a total of 12 active patrols totalling 690 days at sea under three different commanders, and surviving at least 11 different attacks on her from the air and the sea. U-123 was the third most successful U-Boat in terms of merchant tonnage sunk, 219,924 tons, being 42 merchant vessels. This U-Boat also damaged six other merchant ships totalling 53,568 tons, and sank one auxiliary warship of 3,209 tons, and damaged one of 13,984 tons, and also sank one warship of 683 tons.

U-123 left Kiel, Germany on its first active patrol in September 1940, sinking six merchant vessels before arriving at its future home base of Lorient, France. It carried out further sinkings in the North Atlantic but survived an attack by convoy escorts off Portugal involving 126 depth charges, in August 1941.

In January 1942 it commenced Operation Drumbeat off the coast of America where it had its biggest successes sinking over 121,000 tons on two patrols, including a gun battle with the disguised Q Ship USS Atik, losing one of its crew in the exchange. U-123 came very close to being sunk only a week into this new area of operations. On the 19th of January the Norwegian factory whaler Kosmos 11 tried to ram U-123 in shallow water when one of the submarine's engines was not working and she was out of torpedoes. The whaler came within 75 metres before U-123 started her other engine, but it took more than an hour to gradually outrun the whaler and eventually dive to safety.

U-123 continued with further patrols, including the sinking of the Holmbury in May 1943, before being taken out of service in June 1944 and then scuttled in Lorient in August 1944. This submarine was raised by France after the end of the war in 1945 and became the French submarine Blaison (Q165), until she was decommissioned on the 18th of August 1959.

Commander Horst von Schroeter

Born on the 10th of June 1919 at Bieberstein in Saxony, he started general officer training in 1937 and participated in the occupation of Norway in 1940 as a midshipman on the battle cruiser Scharnhorst. After his duties in Norway were over, he was ordered to undergo special submarine training, and he started sea going warfare on U-Boats in April 1941.

Schroeter became 2nd Watch Officer under the daring Commander Reinhard Hardegen on the first patrol by U-123 off the coast of America. He became 1st Watch Officer on the second patrol during the first six months of 1942, before taking over as Commander of this U-Boat in December 1942, aged 23. He carried out four active patrols on U-123 lasting a total of 343 days in the Atlantic, during which he sank seven ships (32,240 tons) including the Holmbury in May 1943, and damaged one (7,068 tons), He was lucky to survive an attack by an R.A.F. Mosquito in November 1943, which killed one and injured two crew on the conning tower, leaving the U-Boat unable to dive.

His command of U-123 coincided with it being taken out of service in June 1944, but he was then involved with the commissioning of the new powerful Type XX1 U-Boat, U-2506, in Hamburg, taking command on the 31st of August 1944. The tide of the war fortunately overtook these deadly submarines becoming fully operational, and during a patrol in Norwegian waters he learnt that the war was over, and he therefore surrendered the U-Boat in Bergen, Norway on the 9th of May 1945. Schroeter's wartime service had earned him several honours including the Iron Cross 1st and 2nd Class, and the Knights Cross.

In 1956 Schroeter joined the Bundesmarine and he became a Rear Admiral in 1971. From 1976 to his retirement in 1979 he was the commander of the NATO Naval Forces in the Baltic Sea approaches, with a rank of Vice Admiral, and as such was the highest-ranking former U-Boat officer in the Bundesmarine. He died on the 27th of July 2006 aged 87.

Bibliography

National Archives Kew:

Arandora Star: BT381/344, BT389/2

Abosso: BT381/479

Heminge: BT381/715, BT389/15/113

Urla: BT381/1481, BT381/891, BT389/31/16

Kingswood: BT381/1537, BT389/17/271

Holmbury: BT381/1941, BT381/2388, BT389/15/221

Fort Capot River: BT381/2686, BT389/13/78

City of Exeter: BT381/3279, BT389/7/108

Fort Connolly: BT381/3611, BT381/3983, BT389/13/96

Empire Dorado: BT381/1222

Sirus: BT381/1378, BT389/27/105

Clan Cumming: BT381/1168, BT389/7/185

Orduna: BT381/2283, BT389/22/297

Gold shipments to USA: CUST 106/197

Loch Ewe: ADM 1/11619

Hull Docks: HO192/1255

Bari Attack: WO204/7759

Seamen Abroad: MT9/3445, MT9/3411, MT9/3714

MN Wireless Use: ADM 1/10190

Board of Trade Shipping Loss Reports for Heminge, Urla and Holmbury

Other Sources:

Bodleian Library, the Marconi Archives, Radio Officer Records

Liverpool Maritime Museum, D/ROE Marconi Radio Officer Exam Results and Morse

Code Training

Imperial War Museum, Samuel Burwell audio 21577

Books:

Marconi - A War Record by George Godwin

Loch Ewe WW2 by George Chadwick

U-Boat Captive by J.B. Lawson

WIMS (Wartime Instructions for Merchant Ships)

Websites:

British Newspaper Archives

Hull Daily Mail

New York Times

U-Boat.net

Arnold Hague Convoy Database

RegiaMarina.net

Merchant-Navy.net

benjidog.co.uk

Hull History Centre

Excerpt from Churchill's speech taken from: New York Times, April 10, 1941 http://www.ibiblio.org/pha/policy/1941/410409a.html

Map showing positions of Urla and Heminge sinkings adapted from: https://map.comersis.com/carte-Atlantic-ocean-blank-editable-map-cm7th1f8ht2.html

Map showing position of Holmbury sinking adapted from: https://d-maps.com/carte.php?num_car=1054&lang=en